BAKING SODA

Over 500 Fabulous, Fun and Frugal Uses You've Probably Never Thought Of

by

VICKI LANSKY

illustrations by Martha Campbell

printed on recycled paper

BOOK PEDDLERS
MINNETONKA, MN

Special thanks to:
Brian Thomlinson, Wayne Sorenson, Cathy Marino, Ray Brown, Gloria Spitz, Jim Levine, Cindy Shellum, and Kathryn Ring

Cover design by Laurie Ingram-Duren
Illustrations by Martha Campbell

ISBN 0-916773-41-8

COPYRIGHT © Vicki Lansky 1995
First Printing March 1995
2nd edition January 2004

Publisher's Cataloging in Publication
(Prepared by Quality Books, Inc)
Lansky, Vicki L.
  Baking soda : over 500 fabulous, fun and frugal uses you've probably never thought of/ Vicki L. Lansky.
    p.cm.
  ISBN 0-916773-41-8

  1. Home economics—Miscellanea. 2 Sodium compounds—Miscellanea.   I. Title.TX158.L36 1995   640.41
                                                    QB194-1795

BOOK PEDDLERS
2828 Hedberg Drive • Minnetonka, MN 55305
952/544-1154 • fax: 952/544-1153
www.bookpeddlers.com • *vlansky@bookpeddlers.com*

PRINTED IN THE UNITED STATES

07 08 09 17 16 15 14

Ode by a Mother to Baking Soda

How do I use thee?
I can't count the ways. . . .
You scrub my tub, presoak my clothes
Freshen my fridge, won't scratch stoves;
Eat odors in sneakers and diaper pails
Soothe bites and burns to stop kids' wails.
All of this without harming our earth,
You give far more than my money's worth.

Jane Fraser, Picton, ONT Canada

Table of Contents

4 IN THE BATHROOM

5 HOME MAINTENANCE

6 LAUNDRY TIME

7 HYGIENE AND GROOMING

8 HOME REMEDIES

9 LITTLE TYKES

10 PLAY PROJECTS FOR KIDS

introduction

Whenever I mentioned to people that I was working on a book of everything you can do with baking soda and that I had over 500 uses, I inevitably caught their attention. First they didn't believe baking soda had more than a handful of uses; second, they would then relate the one or two they knew of or used; and third, they expected me to rattle off a dozen or so ideas right there and then—which I usually did, to their amazement!

Everyone, it seems, is interested in ways baking soda can be used. As a contributing editor to Family Circle Magazine writing about household hints, I was sent lots of great uses for baking soda by readers. In my book, ANOTHER USE FOR...101 COMMON HOUSEHOLD ITEMS, I had three pages alone of "other" uses for baking soda. Browsing through my collection of tips books, newspaper and magazine clippings, I gleaned dozens more. AND THEY ARE ALL HERE.

I have not tested each and every idea here. What I have done is collect what has worked for someone—sometime—and in all probability will work for you. But use common sense. Conditions and situations are unique to each of us. I can not guarantee each and every usage listed. I did want to share all the wonderful ones I know about and let you be the judge of what is useful to you.

The folks at Church & Dwight, Co., Inc, who market ARM & HAMMER® have been kind enough to provide me with information and feedback, but this book has not been written for them. Though they are enthusiastic about the book, they are not responsible for the information printed here.

If I missed a use for baking soda that works for you, do let me know. You can send it to me in care of *the Book Peddlers* or *Practical Parenting.*

— Vicki Lansky

CHAPTER ONE

BAKING SODA

WHAT IT IS,
HOW IT WORKS,
HOW WE USE IT,
and
HOW IT CAME TO BE SO POPULAR

Baking soda is actually sodium bicarbonate (also known as bicarbonate of soda). It is found naturally in mineral deposits, lake sediments and groundwater. It is even found in our oceans where its bicarbonate chemistry seemingly works to stabilize the carbon dioxide content of the earth's atmosphere. Virtually all baking soda in North America today comes from the mined mineral, trona, which can be found in large amounts in one place—Green River, Wyoming. (Other large deposits of trona can be found in Kenya, Egypt, Venezuela and the deserts of Central Asia.) This massive deposit was discovered in the 1930s on federal lands. Trona is actually half sodium bicarbonate and half its chemical cousin, sodium carbonate, some of which ends up as the more familiar *washing soda*. Trona is deep mined as opposed to an open-pit procedure. The ore is brought to the surface, crushed, washed and heated to make sodium carbonate. When this is dissolved in water and carbon dioxide is bubbled through the solution, sodium bicarbonate crystals form and fall out of the solution. These crystals then go through a washing and drying process before the product is packaged and distributed.

Baking soda is manufactured in one other factory—a natural factory: the human body. Here it maintains the correct acidity level (or pH) of the bloodstream. It is found in our saliva, where it neutralizes the plaque acids in our mouth to prevent teeth from dissolving. The same body production of sodium bicarbonate neutralizes stomach acids to help prevent ulcers. It helps people to breathe by carrying carbon dioxide from bodily tissue to the lungs, where it is exhaled. Amazing!

How—and Why—Does It Work?

Baking soda has a few fundamental qualities which overlap:
    1) It has a soft crystalline molecular structure.
    2) It has the ability to neutralize acidity.
    3) It is a leavening agent.
    4) It is able to absorb many odors.

Abrasive Ability

Baking soda's first attribute makes it mildly abrasive, which is why it's known for its gentle yet effective cleaning ability. It is soluble in water, which allows the crystals to "round off" and dissolve before they can scratch or damage a surface.

A Natural Neutralizer

Baking soda's ability to buffer or neutralize acids naturally (keeping the pH as close to neutral as possible) enables it to work in a wide range of seemingly unconnected applications. It can modify kitchen odors before they evaporate and smell bad, as well as neutralize acid corrosion on car battery terminals, and neutralize the acid in mosquito venom which is what causes such bites to itch. Baking soda can even be used to reduce the corrosion of drinking water in municipal water supplies, therefore reducing lead and copper toxicity.

There are many medicinal uses for baking soda. It is used in kidney dialysis to reduce the level of acids in the bloodstream and as an antacid to control acid indigestion. It can even act to prevent microbial growth in food products.

Dirt and grease are usually composed of fatty acids that can be neutralized by baking soda, too. Once neutralized, the fatty acids dissolve in water and can be easily wiped away. Baking soda can neutralize unpleasant airborne odors *(because odors are usually acid-based, much like sour milk smelling bad)* because it chemically neutralizes them too. Baking soda also works on our own body odors, pet urine odors or the mouth-plaque that causes bad-breath. Other products often rely on added fragrances which mask odors; with baking soda such odors are actually gone because the offensive smell has been absorbed.

A Baking Boon

Its leavening abilities in cooking are also rooted in acid-base chemistry. When baking soda is mixed with an acid (such as milk, chocolate, vinegar, lemon juice, or large amounts of honey or molasses) it neutralizes the acid component and releases carbon dioxide air bubbles. This in turn causes the mixture to rise from these carbon dioxide bubbles that are now trapped by the gluten—the stretchy protein in wheat flour.

Not only does it work this way for cakes, muffins and other baked goods—both commercial and homemade—but it can also be used to make brittle candies airy and porous.

Baking soda is often confused with baking powder since they leaven in much the same way. Baking powder, however, is a combination of both baking soda and an acid (such as cream of tartar) with which it will react when added to a liquid. Therefore it works well in recipes that do not include other acid ingredients. Today's double-acting baking powder acts in two ways because it contains two types of acids. One is activated by moisture, the other is activated by heat. The additional tiny air bubbles released during the baking process create a finer texture to baked goods. *(Be aware that too much additional baking powder can result in a "sunken" baked product. Proportions count. This is one situation where "more" is not necessarily better.)*

Other Traits

Baking soda has other uses that are not related to its abrasive, buffering or baking abilities. For one, it works as a fire extinguisher when applied to a grease or electrical fire. It is also used in water softening products because it does just that. It is used for biological and medicinal purposes as an ingredient in over-the-counter and prescription drugs. In the plant care world, it is sometimes used to control the development of mold, fungus and mildew. It is used in animal feed lots. It is blended into feed for cows to maximize milk output so beef cattle maintain their maximum weight gain. It's added to chicken feed to produce tougher egg shells and control the amount of sodium chloride. The list goes on.

In the Beginning...

It was out of need for an affordable, clean, consistent leavening agent in colonial America that a refined sodium bicarbonate—baking soda—was born. To leaven baked products, as mentioned above, one must trap carbon dioxide bubbles in flour to make it to rise. This was usually done by capturing bubbles in the dough by kneading it for long periods of time, using a sourdough as a leavening starter, using yeast to allow bread to rise or by any or all of these methods.

Early on, bakers realized that potassium carbonate—a component of pearlash (a concentrated form of potash)—had leavening qualities. Potash which could be made from the ash of burnt timber which was needed in the manufacture of colonial soap and glass. People discovered that potassium carbonate's alkaline quality reduced the sourness in sourdough bread yet helped it rise. Pearlash now had a new use and was packaged at that time as a product called American Saleratus—saleratus translated meant "aerated salt." It was their way of saying this white powder produced carbon dioxide bubbles that seemed to add "air" and lift to their baking efforts.

A viable commercial method to create soda ash was created in Europe. Two Belgian brothers developed a break-through process in 1863 for making soda ash, which came to bear their name—the Solvay process. Their product was sodium—versus potassium—carbonate. It was introduced from Europe into the American market but was not produced in America until almost twenty years later, when the first Solvay processing plant was built in Syracuse, New York. Solvay plants were only dis-placed when trona mining became predominant after World War II. The last (and also the original) Solvay plant closed in 1984.

In 1839 in upstate New York, a doctor named Austin Church was looking for a way to expand his family's income. This was a time when much of medical training was concentrated on chemistry, and he enjoyed chemical research. Now if a cheaper, more reliable and cleaner "saleratus" could be produced from sodium carbonate, reasoned this early American entrepre-neur, perhaps there was money to be made. He heated soda ash (sodium carbonate) over a wood-burning fire and found that over time, thanks to the moisture and the carbon dioxide from the rising heat, it changed sodium carbonate to sodium bicarbonate. In 1846 Dr. Church was joined in his business venture by John Dwight, his wife's younger brother. They both moved to New York City at that time to begin serious commercial distribution of baking soda in the United States. New York was an ideal spot because it was a port for receiving the raw material and it was a large population center for selling their product. Dr. Church was responsible for the manufacturing; Dwight for sales and market-ing. The first manufacturing and production site for baking soda—the trade name for bicarbonate of soda—was said to be in John Dwight's home where it was packaged in a new innovative consumer form—one pound paper bags with a recognizable red label. The company, called Dwight & Company sold their product as Dwight's Saleratus. Because it was used with sour milk in baking, COW BRAND® was adopted as its trademark.

After a twenty year business association Dr. Austin Church retired, but two years later he returned to develop with his sons a new company and production facility in a partnership that became known as Church & Company. They chose ARM & HAMMER® Brand Bicarbonate of Soda as their trademark identity. The symbol represented the arm of Vulcan—the god of fire, blacksmith of the Roman gods—with the arm of Vulcan holding the hammer in hand preparing to strike the anvil. Obviously they wanted a strong, recognizable image for their product. *(By the way, this name has no relation at all to the successful businessman, Armand Hammer, who made his fortune in the oil market in the second half of the 1900s.)*

Regardless of the fact that both families were competing in the same business, the competition never seemed to overshadow the families' support of each other. These good relations surely helped when, in 1896, the descendants of Dwight & Company and those of Church & Company joined forces, consolidating the companies under the name Church & Dwight, Co., Inc. and chose to use the ARM & HAMMER trademark. It has operated under that name now for over 150 years. As of 1995, Dwight Minton, a fifth generation founding family member wasCEO of the company. The company was still 40 percent owned by its founding families at that time, and employees owned 5 percent of the company stock.

Baking soda was an early, popular American consumer product. Its early success was helped by many factors of its day: a move from open fire cooking to stoves with built-in ovens with controlled heating; the proliferation of American cookbooks; a flourishing flour processing industry; a developing food distribution system that could sell individually packaged products insuring a clean product direct to the consumer; the development of the railroads bringing consumer goods to the West; and consumers finding additional non-food uses for baking soda such as a tooth powder.

The Baking Soda Industry Today

Church & Dwight and ARM & HAMMER® have come to be synonymous with the word baking soda in the United States. They have one of the highest trusted names in the consumer market place today and probably control 90 percent of the market for baking soda at the consumer level. Their product can also be found in Mexico and Great Britain. In Canada the long used Church & Dwight COW® Brand Baking Soda has recently been phased out and replaced with the ARM & HAMMER® Brand. In many other countries, ARM & HAMMER® is an unknown consumer name. In Australia, the product on the shelves is McKenzie's Bi-Carb, and Borthwick's Bicarbonate of Soda is another name you'll find in England.

While Church & Dwight have preempted the consumer market place, they are not the only producers of baking soda. There are other commodity chemical companies that do compete with them in the large and expanding industrial business, and in commercial leavening and the private label market place. Private label packagers who purchase processed baking soda from these commodity companies repackage it as generic baking soda as well as using it as an ingredient in their own private label cake mixes. Bicarbonate of soda is one of the ingredients in pool chemical packages and often comes from these other companies. There are two large and several smaller commodity companies who also lease, mine and refine trona today including FMC, Rhone-Poulenc and Elf-Aquitaine (which owns Texas Gulf). None of these companies market directly to consumers.

In Green River, Wyoming, where trona is mined, Church & Dwight have a processing plant used mainly for their West

Coast distribution. A processing site for their East Coast distribution is in Old Fort, Ohio.

An Environmentally Friendly Product

A resurgent interest in baking soda in the last 20 years developed as the public's interest in using products less harmful to our environment grew. Studies show that baking soda is environmentally benign. Home economists and environmentalists have known this for years and have consistently recommended baking soda as an alternative to the more toxic, harsher chemical cleaners on the market. Certainly the variety of home uses for baking soda have surpassed its home cooking uses long ago.

Because of its environmental friendliness, baking soda has been put to good use in industry, too. Church & Dwight's product, ARMAKLEEN®, is used to replace CFCs-chlorofluoro-carbons, an ozone depleting chemical—formerly used in the manufacturing of electronic circuit boards, for one.

Church & Dwight also pioneered the use of sodium bicarbonate in industrial applications that protect the air and water by reducing lead contamination in drinking water, removing acid gas from smoke stack emissions and removing paint and grime without the use of chemical solvents. The highest profile use of their commercial product called ARMEX BLAST MEDIA®—a low abrasion blasting product—used in graffiti removal, was to clean the interior surfaces of the Statue of Liberty in its recent restoration.

Today Church & Dwight have expanded their product line to include toothpaste (ARM & HAMMER® Dental Care), carpet deodorizer, an anti-perspirant deodorant, cat litter deodorizer and a low-phospate and phosphate-free laundry detergent, amongst others. Their introduction of toothpaste with baking soda that neutralizes plaque acids was so successful that other companies have jumped on their bandwagon. The Wall Street Journal reports that even though there are no scientific reports to support the hypothesis that baking soda is better for teeth than regular toothpaste, dentists still recommend its use. *(The baking soda mystique is so strong that one company has even developed a baking soda dental floss!)*

A Company with an Environmental Conscience

Even in the beginning days of the company, Church & Dwight was a politically correct company, though more by accident than design, as early management included bird and wildlife enthusiasts. Over a hundred years ago they chose wildlife conservation as the basis of their first marketing efforts. Offers of small trading cards of birds, animals, fish and wildflowers appeared on their boxes—an innovative marketing plan in itself—to build a loyal consumer following. In the 1920s a senior officer of the company commissioned original artwork for additional cards. On the back of the cards that depicted yellow warblers, scarlet tanagers and purple finches were the words, FOR THE GOOD OF ALL, DO NOT DESTROY THE BIRDS.

Today there is the position of Director of Public Affairs and Environmental Management in the corporate offices of Church & Dwight, Inc. in Princeton, New Jersey. This company, which remains the major consumer and industrial producer of baking soda today, monitors all aspects of its own business as it relates to protecting the environment from internal pollution prevention to external life-cycle analysis of its own products. Their own boxes, for instance, have used recycled paper for more than 80 years.

Enough said. Let's turn to the more important business at hand—how baking soda can be put to use in your life in more ways than you ever thought possible.

If you wish to keep current with offers from ARM & HAMMER®
and you have access to the Internet, add this address to your Book
Marks/Favorite Places spot on your computer:
http://www.armhammer.com

WAYS BAKING SODA CAN BE USED

1) In an OPEN BOX
Remove the top of a box of baking soda and place it where needed to reduce odors. *(For additional open box ideas, see page 37). (Also, there is the new ARM & HAMMER® package made with vents to act as an "open" box.)*

2) In SOLUTION
Use from 4 tablespoons in 1 quart warm water to 1/2 box in a full bathtub.

3) As a PASTE
Add just enough water or other indicated liquid to whatever amount you are using to create a paste.

4) As a SPRINKLE-ON
Apply lightly to a damp cloth or sponge, or directly on area by hand or from a container or dispenser.
(For container ideas, see page 36.)

CHAPTER TWO

COOKING TIPS

When it comes to baking soda, most of us think of baking as its primary function, so we'll start here. But there are lots of other cooking uses you'll find interesting and helpful.

Baking Tips

- Give a chocolate cake a darker texture by mixing 1 teaspoon baking soda with the other dry ingredients

- Keep icing moist and prevent its cracking by adding a pinch of baking soda before spreading it on a cake.

- Make your own self-rising flour by combining:
  - 3-1/2 cups flour
  - 1-3/4 teaspoons baking powder
  - 1-3/4 teaspoons baking soda
  - 1-3/4 teaspoons salt

- Sweeten tart blackberries for pies and cobblers by adding 1/2 teaspoon baking soda before adding sugar.

- Consider adding baking soda to your dry ingredients when combining baking ingredients as your SOP (*Standard Operating Procedure*)!

- For perfect sour cream pound cake, add the baking soda to the sour cream before you start mixing the cake ingredients. The soda is activated in the sour cream to begin its work earlier.

- Mix batters quickly and put them in a preheated oven fairly fast so that gases don't escape from the dough before baking. Remember, the leavening action is a result of the reaction between the acid ingredient and the alkaline baking soda. When these ingredients are combined they give off the carbon dioxide bubbles. This reaction starts when the dry ingredients are combined with the wet ones as the acid component is usually in the wet ingredient.

- Make fluffy breakfast biscuits without yeast by substituting 1 teaspoon baking soda and an equal amount of ascorbic acid (or powdered vitamin C) for the yeast called for. No need to let the dough rise; that will occur during the baking process.

BEST CHOCOLATE CHIP COOKIE RECIPE

2-1/4 cups flour
1 teaspoon baking soda
3/4 teaspoon salt
1 cup shortening (margarine or butter, softened)
3/4 cup granulated sugar
3/4 cup packed brown sugar
1 teaspoon vanilla flavoring
2 eggs
2 cups (12 ounces) semi-sweet chocolate chips
1 cup chopped nuts, optional

Mix flour, baking soda and salt in one bowl. In a larger bowl, combine shortening, sugars and vanilla until creamy. Beat in eggs. Gradually add dry ingredients and mix well. Stir in chocolate chips and nuts, if using.

Drop by rounded teaspoonfuls onto an ungreased cookie sheet. Bake at 375°F about 8 minutes or until lightly browned. Makes about 2 dozen 2-inch cookies.

Substituting Honey for Sugar?

• To substitute honey for sugar in a cake, cookie, or quick bread recipe, use 2/3 cup honey for each cup of sugar. Then add 1/2 teaspoon baking soda for every cup of honey used (to neutralize the acidity). Reduce the liquid in the recipe by 1/4 cup and bake at a temperature 25°F lower than the recipe calls for to prevent over-browning.

TESTING FOR BAKING SODA FRESHNESS
Pour a small amount of vinegar or lemon juice—a few drops will do—over 1/2 teaspoon of baking soda. If it doesn't bubble actively—it's too old.

Baking soda is usually used in place of baking powder in recipes involving sour milk or some other acid, like molasses or honey. If the dough contains a natural acidic ingredient such as sour milk, buttermilk, yogurt, chocolate or molasses, baking soda is usually the lone leavening ingredient you need. As a rule of thumb, 1/2 teaspoon baking soda will be used for every 1 cup "acidic ingredient" called for. While it may seem redundant, you'll note that many recipes call for both baking soda and baking powder. The additional baking soda can help get the action working sooner and often promotes the browning of the surface of cakes, cookies or muffins.

Baking Powder Pointers
Baking powder is simply baking soda with a dry acid added so that it activates the baking soda when it becomes moist and/or is heated. For many years cream of tartar *(as the needed acidic ingredient)* combined with baking soda was the commercial baking product sold. Today commercial baking powder is packaged with citric acid powder or sodium aluminum phosphate or other baking "acids."

Out of baking powder? Make your own by substituting any of the following:
  1) To make one teaspoon of baking powder:
   1/4 teaspoon baking soda plus 3/8 teaspoon cream of tartar
   or
   1/4 teaspoon baking soda plus 1/2 cup sour milk
   or
   1/4 teaspoon baking soda plus 1/2 teaspoon vinegar, or lemon juice and 1/2 cup sweet milk.

2) The right proportion to 1 cup flour is:
>1 teaspoon baking soda
>2 teaspoons cream of tartar
>1/2 teaspoon salt

3) Or combine:
>1 tablespoon baking soda
>1 tablespoon cream of tartar
>1 tablespoon cornstarch

Don't store homemade baking powder. Commercial brands contain small amounts of ingredients such as flour to prevent absorption of moisture from the air which would cause a loss of its leavening powers. *(That's the reason baking powder comes in an air tight container.)*

Test baking powder's effectiveness by mixing 1 teaspoon baking powder with 1/3 cup hot water. If it bubbles actively then it is still fresh enough to use.

Stove Top Secrets

• To make a fluffy omelette, add 1/2 teaspoon baking soda for every 3 eggs.

• Add a pinch of baking soda to buttermilk (used instead of whole milk) to make waffles light and soft.

• Add fluff to your mashed potatoes with a pinch of baking soda during mashing.

• A pinch of baking soda added to any boiled syrup will prevent crystallizing.

• Avoid curdling boiled milk by adding a pinch of baking soda.

• When gravy separates add a pinch or two of baking soda to emulsify those fat globules in seconds.

Main Course Magic

- Tenderize tough meat by rubbing it with baking soda. Let it stand for several hours before rinsing and cooking.

- Use a bit of baking soda in the water in which you clean the insides and outsides of poultry. Rinse with clean water. There's no residue to worry about.

- Rub baking soda into the fat surrounding pork chops to make them extra crispy.

- Soak raw fish for at least a half hour in 2 tablespoons baking soda and 1 quart water. Rinse and pat dry before cooking. The fishy taste will disappear.

- Try adding 1 teaspoon baking soda to potato pancakes to help cure indigestion for people who cannot tolerate regular fried potato pancakes or any fried foods.

- Add a pinch of baking soda to Swiss fondue just before serving to bind all the ingredients together.

Wild Ideas

- Tenderize fowl by rubbing the inside with baking soda, then refrigerating it overnight.

- When scalding an unplucked chicken add 1 teaspoon baking soda to the boiling water. Feathers are said to come off more easily and the skin will be clean.

- Remove the wild taste from game meat by soaking it in baking soda and water overnight in your refrigerator. Rinse well and pat dry before cooking.

- After field-dressing a deer, sprinkle baking soda in the cavities to control odors until you can get the meat processed.

Vegamatic

- Clean dirt and residue off fresh fruit and vegetables by sprinkling baking soda on a wet sponge and scrubbing away. Rinse with water.

- Avoid over cooking cabbage and make it more tender by cooking it in water with a pinch of baking soda added.

- Add 1 teaspoon baking soda to the water when you cook cauliflower to keep the vegetable snowy white and cut cooking odors.

- A bit of baking soda will usually intensify the color of all steamed vegetables. (*Some feel adding baking soda destroys some vitamins and nutrients and that it's better to add vinegar or lemon juice to stabilize color.*)

- Remove the bitter taste when cooking turnip or mustard greens by adding 1/2 teaspoon baking soda to the cooking water.

- Try adding a dash of baking soda to baked beans to eliminate gaseous side effects.

- Wash your fruits and vegetables in a large bowl of cool water to which you've added 2 to 3 tablespoons of baking soda. This, many feel, helps remove pesticides as well as any dirt and wax.

- Cover fresh cranberries with water and bring to a boil. Add 1 teaspoon baking soda, stir, drain and return pan to the burner. Then add sugar to the now-soft berries and finish cooking. Cranberries require less added sugar this way.

- Cut down on the amount of sugar needed in rhubarb sauce by soaking the rhubarb in cold water and a pinch of baking soda prior to cooking. The water will turn black. Drain off this water, add fresh water and cook. The sauce gets sweet with less sugar because you've lowered the acidity of the rhubarb.

• Sprinkle a bit of baking soda on freshly sliced pineapple for a tasty treat, especially if the fruit is not quite ripe.

Tomato Savvy
• Add a pinch of baking soda to a pot of tomato-based spaghetti sauce or chili to cut the acidity level.

• Moisten a teaspoon and dip the tip into baking soda. Stir home or commercially canned tomatos with the spoon. If the tomatos bubble, their acidic level is high. The baking soda also removes some of the acidity. (*Some tomatos today have been bred with reduced acidic levels.*)

• Keep homemade cream of tomato soup from curdling by adding a pinch of baking soda before you add the tomatoes.

Whoops!
• If you've added too much vinegar to a recipe, add a pinch of baking soda to counteract the excess acidity.

• Out of yeast? Substitute equal parts baking soda and powdered Vitamin C or citric acid. This dough does not need to rise before baking. (*This combination is a form of a homemade baking powder you can use in place of yeast to help dough rise.*)

• Avoid lumping of baking soda in batter by mixing the soda with 1 teaspoon vinegar. The vinegar reacts with the baking soda to dissolve lumps!

Drinks Ahoy
• Soften boiled drinking water with 1 teaspoon baking soda per gallon.

• Make your own low-acid coffee. Add a pinch of baking soda to a cup of your regular coffee. This small amount won't alter the taste. *(This tip works with other high-acid foods too, and may be useful for some medical conditions that require a low-acid diet, such as ulcers or interstitial cystitis.)*

• Get more from tea bags by adding a pinch of baking soda to the teapot while steeping the tea, and your tea won't cloud. This works for iced as well as hot tea.

• Add 1/4 teaspoon baking soda to an 8-ounce glass of orange juice, grapefruit juice or lemonade and stir well, to make an interesting-looking fizzy drink for children or adults. The acidity level of the juice will also be cut.

CHAPTER THREE

KITCHEN CARE

No doubt the kitchen is where you currently have at least one box of baking soda and you're going to be surprised at all the ways you can use it—just in your kitchen—other than for cooking!

Counter Measures

• Be aware that stains on Formica and other plastic laminates respond best to the bleaching quality of freshly squeezed lemon juice. Leave the juice on for a half hour, then sprinkle with baking soda. Scrub with a cloth, rinse, and dry. This process works well for both shiny and dull-finish Formicas.

• Make cuts in a countertop seem to fade away by keeping them clean with a paste of baking soda and water.

• Remove ink marks from food price stamps on counters with a little baking soda and water paste. It also removes many stains left from tea bags, juice spills and mustard dabs.

• Give cutting boards regular, deep cleaning to keep them free from contamination. Spread baking soda over the surface, then sprinkle liberally with vinegar. Let the bubbles do their thing, then rinse with hot water.

• Or just sprinkle baking soda on a damp sponge and rub into wood and other porous surfaces to remove onion, garlic and other food odors. Rinse with clear water.

• Keep dry baking soda in a pretty bowl near your sink. Just dip the edge of a wet cloth or sponge in it to clean up stains.

• Or store it in a large shaker.

A Homemade Scouring Powder

Combine the following for a premixed cleaning powder:

   1 cup baking soda
   1 cup borax
   1 cup salt

Use as you would any commercial scouring powder.

- Clean and shine a toaster oven with baking soda and warm water. Or try polishing the chrome with a paste of equal parts peanut butter and baking soda. (*Creamy peanut butter preferred!*) We're told your toaster will shine!

- Clean a blender by first filling it half-full of water. Add 1 teaspoon baking soda and 1 drop detergent. Secure lid and turn on the blender briefly. Rinse clean.

- Rid your hands of the odor of onions and garlic by sprinkling baking soda in the palm of one hand. Add just enough water to make a paste, rub this paste between your hands and rinse off.

Under the Counter

- Sprinkle baking soda inside your rubber gloves. They'll slide on easily, keep dry, and smell good.

- Prevent steel wool scouring pads from rusting after each use by storing them in a container filled with a solution of baking soda and water.

- Keep your in-use dish towels smelling fresh by sprinkling baking soda on them and shaking off the excess in the sink before putting them away.

Sink Savers

- Cut grease and speed removal of sticky foods on dishes and utensils by adding baking soda to hot, sudsy dishwater. Use from 1 tablespoon to 1 cup, depending upon the amount of water you're using.

- After washing dishes, soak your dishcloth or sponge in baking soda and water. Swish the sink with the soda solution and then wring out the cloth or sponge and everything will be sweet and odor-free.

- At canning time, 1 tablespoon baking soda added to the boiling water bath before you discard it, keeps your kitchen sink smelling fresh.

- Use baking soda as a wonderful nonabrasive cleanser for stainless-steel sinks, which can be scratched by even some liquid cleansers.

- Whiten porcelain sinks by covering the surface area with a cloth dishtowel or paper towels and pour on just enough bleach to saturate the cloths. Let set for 5 to 10 minutes. Pick up the towels, rinse sink and cloth towels with water then sprinkle baking soda over the sink. Clean the sink with a sponge or the freshened wet dishcloth to remove bleach residue and smell.

Drain Cleaner

- Help open a clogged drain by pouring 1 cup baking soda down the drain and then adding 1 cup hot vinegar. *(Your microwave is perfect for heating the vinegar.)* Wait a few minutes before flushing the drain with about a quart of very hot water. Repeat if necessary. This method of cleaning and deodorizing drains avoids using harsh chemicals and is therefore kinder to the environment. This process, cutting down to 1/4 cup baking soda and 1/2 cup vinegar, is also excellent for keeping garbage disposals clean.

- Or pour 1/2 cup each—baking soda and salt—down the drain, followed by 1 cup boiling water. Let this set over night and flush with hot tap water the next morning. *(You can keep a premixed container of 1 pound—a 16-oz. box—baking soda and 1 pound table salt together in an air tight container and use as needed.)*

- Use up any baking soda you've determined is no longer fresh and has absorbed odors by storing it with your general cleaning supplies. *(Don't use this box for cooking needs.)* Drains, especially in the kitchen, profit from a good baking soda rinse on a regular basis even without vinegar.

- Remove hard water stains on faucets with a paste of toothpaste and baking soda. Scrub with an old toothbrush, then rinse.

- Before leaving on vacation, pour some baking soda down the kitchen drain and disposal *(no need to run any water)* to cancel any possible future odors.

Automatic Dishwasher Power

- Create your own dishwasher detergent by mixing 2 table-spoons baking soda with 2 tablespoons borax.

- Sprinkle a handful of baking soda over dirty dishes—loaded but not washed—and in the bottom of your dishwasher to absorb odors. This extra baking soda will take the place of detergent in your first cycle so you only need to add detergent to the second cycle dispenser.

- Freshen your dishwasher by adding 1/2 box baking soda and running the dishwasher just through a rinse cycle.

- Sprinkle baking soda inside the dishwasher before you leave on vacation. Leave your machine open just a crack and you won't come home to musty smells!

Glass and Plastic

- Make good crystal really sparkle by giving it a short soaking in baking soda and warm water.

- Clean vinegar and oil cruets with baking soda. Shake and allow the baking soda to absorb the oils in the bottle. Rinse clean.

- Make scratch marks in stoneware less visible by applying a thick paste of baking soda and water to them. Let set for a few minutes before washing the dishes as usual.

- Clean baby bottles with baking soda. No danger of soap residue, and you're combatting the possibility of odor buildup. (See page 72 for additional baby cleaning ideas.)

- Use a paste of baking soda as a scouring cleaner with a rag or sponge to scrub plastic bowls. Nothing cleans plastic as well as baking soda, and it won't scratch the surface.

- Remove odors from plastic refrigerator food storage containers. Fill them with very hot water, add 1 tablespoon baking soda, a few drops liquid detergent and 1 tablespoon vinegar. Let set for 5 to 15 minutes—maybe even overnight—before rinsing clean.

- Fill vacuum and regular water bottles with 1 or 2 tablespoons baking soda and water and let them stand for a while to keep stale odors from collecting—especially those from milk. Swish the solution or sponge out the interiors. A dash of lemon juice will also help wipe out coffee stains.

- Odor lingering? Sprinkle some baking soda in the cleaned plastic bowl as though you were dusting a cake pan. Cover with its top and leave overnight. Next day, shake out excess baking soda and wipe the bowl clean.

Brewing Up the Best

- Rid teapots and coffee pots of their mineral deposits by bringing a solution of a cup of vinegar and 4 tablespoons baking soda to a boil, then simmer for a few minutes.

- Keep any coffeemaker clean by brewing up 1 quart warm water and 1/4 cup baking soda. Doing this regularly will keep your coffee tasting great.

• Clean a coffee filter basket or permanent filter by first wetting it, then covering the inside with baking soda. Let it set for a while before brushing it clean with a vegetable brush or old toothbrush to get in the crevices. Rinse well.

• Clean a Corningware teapot by filling it with water to which you've added 1 tablespoon baking soda. Bring to a boil and rinse clean.

• Remove rust stains and mineral deposits from teapots by filling them with water, 2 tablespoons baking soda and the juice of half a lemon. Boil gently for 15 minutes. Rinse. Repeat if needed.

• Make a paste of baking soda to remove tea and coffee stains from cups. Rub it on with your fingertip, a soft damp cloth or a sponge.

Fridge Freshness

• Every refrigerator—and freezer— can profit from an open box of baking soda in it to guard against unwanted and stale odors. The manufacturer recommends replacing the current box with a fresh one every three months. One way to remember is to change boxes with the first day of the season: summer, fall, winter and spring. Of course you can also date the box.

• Fridge odor won't disappear? It actually might be an over-worked, extinct box of baking soda itself. Toss it and start fresh.

• Deodorize heavy-duty bad smells such as spoiled meat by washing the inside walls and shelves of the refrigerator with baking soda and putting in a new box. If that doesn't do it, the other odor absorbers to try are: dry coffee grounds, a bowl with pieces of barbecue charcoal or a few fabric softener sheets.

• Use "sachets" mentioned on page 37 for your refrigerator. Put them in different sections.

• Fight stagnant odors in the water-collecting tray under your refrigerator by sprinkling it generously with baking soda each time you clean it.

• Sprinkle baking soda in crisper bins to keep them smelling fresh. Cover the layer of baking soda with a paper towel. Replace this every three months, writing the date on the paper towel.

• Remove rust streaks and food residue inside your refrigerator with a paste of baking soda and water. Most stains will vanish.

• Clean and deodorize your defrosted—or frost-free—freezer and refrigerator by washing all sides with a mixture of 4 tablespoons baking soda to 2 quarts of water.

Microwave Tips

• Use a general cleaning solution of 4 tablespoons baking soda to 1 quart warm water for wiping clean the inside surfaces of your microwave oven.

• Consider storing an open or vented container of baking soda right in your microwave to eliminate odors between cleaning and to be available right where you need it for quick cleanups. *(Be sure to remove it before cooking.)*

• Or keep baking soda in a pretty cup so it looks attractive on the counter while food is cooking in the microwave. Put the cup back in the microwave when the food is removed and the oven is off.

• Boil a few spoonfuls of baking soda in a microwave-safe cup with water for 3 to 5 minutes. The insides of the now-damp walls of the microwave oven will be easy to wipe down with a sponge or paper towel.

A Fire-Extinguisher-in-a-Box

Keep a large, opened box of baking soda near the kitchen stove to sprinkle on or toss by handfuls at the base of any flare-ups. If it's an electrical fire, water won't stop it. If it's a grease fire, water will spread it. Baking soda is appropriate to use for either type of fire.

If food is salvageable, just rinse off the baking soda. It will not hurt the food that was cooking.

If you're not comfortable with an open box, keep baking soda in an attractive jar, canister or shaker on the counter near the kitchen stove or oven so it's always handy for extinguishing grease fires.

WARNING: Baking soda should be used only to extinguish SMALL fires. Don't use it on fires in deep fat fryers, as the grease could spatter and spread the flames. It is not a substitute for a commercial fire extinguisher—or for a call to the fire department.

Stove Top Clean Up

- Corning and other glass stovetops keep their original finish when cleaned with baking soda and water in solution or as a paste. Use an old toothbrush to get into tight corners.

- Unclog burners on a gas stove by boiling them in a strong baking soda solution, such as 1/4 box to 2 quarts water.

- Remove cooking oil easily from your stovetop with a solution of white vinegar and baking soda.

- Sprinkle the bottom tray of your toaster oven with a teaspoon of baking soda to eliminate the burnt smell from drippings and crumbs.

- Attack burned on food splatters on the stove top by wetting areas first, then sprinkling them liberally with dry baking soda and letting this sit for a while before wiping up. Repeat as necessary. Be sure there's enough water here to soak into the burned food areas.

- Keep just a little baking soda in the shallow drip pans under gas burners. The soda deodorizes and minimizes any possibility of grease drippings catching on fire.

Disaster Detail

- Bring 2 inches of water to a boil in a pan with a burned bottom. Turn off the heat, add 1/2 cup baking soda and let the pan set overnight. It should clean up easily in the morning.

- Remove really stubborn, cooked-on grease spots by sprinkling the pan with 1/2 cup baking soda, then pouring on an equal amount of vinegar. Let the pan soak for several hours or overnight.

- Or add 1 tablespoon each baking soda and vinegar to 1 cup water and boil away the particles.

- Clean deep oil fryer with baking soda. The gentle abrasive action won't damage the finish; it will absorb residual oils and neutralize odors.

Oven Cleaner

- Remove major oven spills easily by sprinkling them with baking soda when they are still fresh. Let them set for a while, then sponge with warm, soapy water.

- Leave 1 cup plain ammonia in a cold, closed oven overnight. In the morning remove the ammonia, sprinkle baking soda on the oven surfaces and wipe down with paper towels dampened with water. Most of the residue will come off.

- Try baking soda, vinegar, and a scrub pad for a winning combination for a clean oven.

- Or a paste of baking soda and elbow grease alone has been known to do the job!

- Clean glass oven or toaster oven doors by covering them with baking soda and rubbing with paper towels until the grease is absorbed. If the door is really grimy, sprinkle baking soda on the surface, cover it with a wet paper towel and let it "soak" for a while first. Wipe the glass clean with a damp cloth.

Appliances

- Cleanup white appliances that are showing signs of yellowing by applying a solution of 1/4 cup baking soda and 4 cups warm water with a sponge. Let set for 10 minutes before rinsing and drying thoroughly.

- Wash appliance exteriors with a mixture of:
      1/4 cup baking soda
      1/2 cup clear vinegar
      1 cup ammonia
      1 gallon hot water

Greasy Kid Stuff

• Clean wire mesh filters on range hoods by immersing them in a pan of hot water. Pour on baking soda and watch the grease float away.

• Clean oven and grill racks by placing them in a plastic garbage bag outside. Mix 1 cup baking soda and 1/2 cup ammonia and pour over racks in the bag. Tie it with a twist tie and leave it outside overnight. The racks will wipe clean in the morning.

• Or lay racks on a path or driveway. Sprinkle with baking soda and leave them there overnight. The next day they should wash clean easily with hot water.

• De-grease and clean barbecue grills by applying baking soda as a paste with a wire brush. Let set for 15 minutes, then wipe clean and let the grill fire burn away any residue before adding food to the grill's surface.

A Piece from the Past

AN OLD FASHIONED CLEANING MIXTURE RECIPE

Mix 1 ounce of baking soda, 1 ounce of prepared chalk, 1 ounce of pumice stone and 1 ounce of sifted wood ashes. Apply this mixture with a piece of raw white potato.

—from *Household Discoveries: An Encyclopaedia of Practical Recipes and Processes* by Sidney Morse, *copyright 1908*

Making Pots and Pans Shine

- Clean a roasting pan by first generously coating surface with baking soda. Then combine 3/4 cup hot water and 1/4 cup vinegar, and pour it onto the soda. It should fizz the pan clean.

- Eliminate holdover odors and taste of food residue in non-stick fry pans by gently scrubbing them with a paste of baking soda and water. Its low abrasive quality prevents it from harming the finish.

- Remove stains from non-stick pans by boiling in them a solution of 2 tablespoons baking soda, 1 cup water and 1/2 cup bleach for 5 to 10 minutes. Wash and rinse the pans thoroughly before reconditioning with salad oil.

- Or use 2 to 3 tablespoons baking soda with enough water to cover the area and simmer clean. *(Be careful to not let it boil dry.)* Add a lemon slice to the pot to aid the cleaning process.

- Clean a white enamel pot by boiling a generous amount of baking soda and water in it for about 10 minutes. Or scrub the pot with a paste of baking soda and water.

- Clean waffle iron grids with baking soda and a stiff brush or toothbrush to remove food residue so your waffles will be less likely to stick the next time round.

- Reclaim the luster of copper pots by sprinkling them with baking soda and then pouring vinegar over them. Let pots stand for 15 minutes before rinsing clean, or use half a lemon as your scrub brush. Sprinkle baking soda on copper pot bottoms you want to clean and rub them with the half lemon. Rinse and dry.

- Or sprinkle baking soda directly on a half lemon to scrub away at brass and copper pieces.

> *WARNING: Be aware that baking soda can clean aluminum pans but it may also darken them.*

A Silver Lining

- Treat tarnished silverware by placing it on a square of aluminum foil in your sink or in a plastic dishpan, or in an aluminum pan *(foil then not needed)*. Cover the pieces lightly with baking soda and add hot water to cover the item(s). Let this sit for 5 to 15 minutes and the silverware will regain its luster. Or you can use one teaspoon of baking soda and one teaspoon of salt with the hot water and a piece of foil as described above. Rinse items clean in hot water. Wipe with a soft cloth. Note that this will also remove tarnish from patterned crevices, reducing the contrasts, which you may NOT want to have happen. *(P.S. Many feel this is not a good "polishing" method; others swear by it!)*

- Remove tarnish from silver by applying a paste of 1-1/2 tablespoons water and 1/4 cup baking soda with a damp sponge. Rinse and buff dry.

- Bring back the shine in silver by rubbing it with a piece of raw potato dipped in baking soda.

Keeping Rust at Bay

- Remove rust from appliances and linoleum floors with a paste of baking soda and water.

- Remove rust from nuts and bolts by covering them first with baking soda, then pouring vinegar over them and allowing them to set until bubbling action stops. Scrub with a brush.

- Make a paste of one tablespoon baking soda and one teaspoon water. With a damp cloth, wipe this paste onto metal chair or table legs. Scrub lightly with a piece of aluminum foil. Wipe clean with a paper towel.

Garbage Cans
- Neutralize odors in a kitchen garbage can by sprinkling baking soda in the bottom of the can before you insert a plastic liner.

- Fight odors under your sink by placing an open box of baking soda in the areas that are susceptible to smells.

- Sprinkle 1 tablespoon or so of baking soda in a trash compactor three or four times during the course of filling and compacting, to eliminate unwanted odors.

- When adding newspaper to the bottom of a paper bag to catch drips and give it strength, sprinkle in some baking soda so it will also absorb excess odors.

(IN)Dispensable Containers
Create your own. Have more than one. Keep them in different places. Just don't bake or cook with soda you've used for deodorizing, nor use it then as an antacid or for toothbrushing.

SHAKERS:
- Keep baking soda in a flour shaker. It looks good and fits into cabinet space, in both kitchen and bathroom.

- Put baking soda in an empty talcum powder shaker. Adding a few marbles will prevent caking and make sprinkling easier.

- Reuse an empty plastic cleanser container by adding baking soda and re-labeling it. Don't keep this with your baking supplies, please.

- Use a cheese shaker for a dispenser. A crystal one can be especially attractive on a fancy bathroom vanity counter.

- Cover a box of baking soda with attractive self-stick paper (solid or print), punch a few holes in the top and you'll have a convenient and coordinated dispenser to use for cleanups in the kitchen, bathroom or anywhere.

EXPOSURE DEODORIZERS:
• Create an allergy-free "soda sachet" by placing 1/3 cup or less of baking soda in the center of a 6-inch circle of fabric, a coffee filter or a pretty tissue. Gather the top and secure with a ribbon, a twist tie or a rubber band.

• Fill a plastic margarine tub or small yogurt container with baking soda. Replace the lid and punch holes in it.

• Fill a cardboard shoebox—decorated or not—with baking soda. Punch holes in the top and place where needed.

• Make "sachets" by putting a 1/2 cup baking soda in the toes of a pair of old, used clean pantyhose. Tie two knots, one at the fill of the soda and a second one about an inch above the first. Repeat until you run out of hose. Cut between the knots and store these in an air tight container. Use them when you need space-saving, deodorizer "containers." Toss them in with your laundry in the washer when their life cycle is over.

• Fill the toes of old hose or knee-highs with baking soda to make larger "sachet" balls. Secure with a twist tie, a ribbon or just a knot.

• Just punch holes in the top of boxes of baking soda.

   In 1994 ARM & HAMMER® began to market a 20-ounce Fridge-Freezer Pack™ which has non-spill vents on three sides of the box that so you don't have to remove the box top.

CHAPTER FOUR

IN THE BATHROOM

It's time to come clean—which really means keeping an extra supply of baking soda in your bathroom!

Surface Savvy

- Keep a bottle of this homemade bathroom cleanser conveniently located in a spray bottle, ready to work for you.
  Combine:
  > 3 tablespoons baking soda
  > 1/4 cup ammonia
  > 2 cups warm water

- Or, if you choose not to use ammonia, try this.
  Combine:
  > 16-oz (1 lb.) box baking soda
  > 4 tablespoons dishwashing liquid
  > 1 cup warm water

  Pour baking soda into a medium-sized bowl. Add water and mix until mixture is smooth, and pour into a squeeze bottle. Shake well before each use.

- Create your own tile cleanser to use with a brush or sponge.
  Mix:
  > 1/4 cup baking soda
  > 1/2 cup white vinegar
  > 1 cup ammonia
  > 1 gallon warm water

- Clean bathroom grout with a paste of baking soda and warm water. Scrub grout with an old toothbrush. Add a little chlorine bleach to the paste if mold is particularly heavy.

> *WARNING*: Never mix chlorine bleach with ammonia. The combination can create dangerous fumes.

- Apply a baking soda and white vinegar paste to stained marble to make it look maaarvelous!

Tub Sparklers

- Old, porous bathroom tubs or sinks clean well with a paste of baking soda and hydrogen peroxide or of baking soda and ammonia. Let the paste sit for a while before rubbing.

- Rinse stains on non-skid tub appliques or built-in strips with water and sprinkle liberally with baking soda. Let set for a while, scrub, and rinse again.

- Glide your way to a shiny tub surface. Sprinkle baking soda around on the tub's surface. Then stand on two damp sponges or washcloths and let your feet do the work. *(Careful, please!)*

- Saturate a cloth with vinegar before sprinkling baking soda on the tub. Then clean fiberglass tub with the cloth—no elbow grease needed! Rinse well and wipe dry for a spotless shine.

- Add 2 tablespoons baking soda to your bath water and you won't have to worry about ring-around-the-tub! Your bath water will be soft, too.

Shower Secrets

- Pour 1/4 cup baking soda and 1 cup vinegar into a strong, sandwich-sized plastic bag and tie it onto and over a scummy shower head. Let the bubbling brew set for an hour. Remove the bag, then turn on the water. Hard water build-up will be gone and your shower head will sparkle again.

- Remove hard water spots, mildew and rust stains from fiberglass shower stalls without scratching the surface. Sprinkle baking soda on a sponge and scrub away. Rinse and wipe dry. *(The shower drain will smell fresh, too.)*

- Clean tiled shower surfaces by sprinkling baking soda on the surfaces before scrubbing with a nylon netting sponge and some inexpensive shampoo. Rinse clean. *(Make this cleanup part of the end of your own shower routine occasionally.)*

- Clean shower stall doors by first spraying them with clear vinegar. Let it set for a few minutes, then scour with a sponge sprinkled with baking soda. Rinse and wipe or squeegee dry.

Curtain Time

- Wash mildewed or dirty plastic shower curtains in your washing machine on the gentle cycle with two bath towels. Add 1/2 cup baking soda and your detergent during the wash cycle and 1 cup vinegar during the rinse cycle. Let the curtain drip dry.

Potty Power

- Sprinkle 1/2 box of soda into the toilet tank each month and let stand overnight before flushing. The tank and the bowl will both be clean.

- Or sprinkle baking soda liberally into the toilet bowl and scrub with a toilet brush, paying special attention to stains. Let set for 5 minutes before flushing to take advantage of the cleaning power.

- Combine baking soda with just enough vinegar to create a bubbling paste and use it to scrub out toilet bowl stains with a brush.

Air Fresheners

- Use a deodorizer container (see page 37) on top of the toilet tank or on the floor behind it to act as an air freshener. This can be done simply by putting baking soda into an attractive, open bathroom accessory dish you leave out in plain sight.

- Mix equal parts baking soda and your favorite perfumed bath salts for an effective air freshener.

CHAPTER FIVE

HOME MAINTENANCE

Windows, walls, floors, carpets and countertops...any surface can benefit from the wise and careful use of baking soda. "Recipes" and instructions abound.

Window Wonders

- Make the dirtiest window sparkle by washing it with a wet sponge sprinkled with a bit of baking soda. Rinse window with a clean sponge, and dry.

- Wash venetian blinds in a tub of warm water to which you've added 3/4 cup baking soda. Let blinds soak for a half hour before scrubbing with a bath brush. Hold up and rinse with a shower hose and hang to dry. If you hand-rub the cords with some baking soda you will get snowy white results.

- Clean aluminum window and door screens by dipping a wet brush in baking soda and scrubbing. Rinse clean with a sponge or hose.

Wood Workers

- Clean woodwork, walls, appliances with a mixture of:
  1/2 cup vinegar
  1/4 cup baking soda
  1 gallon warm water

If the surfaces are really greasy, consider adding 1 cup ammonia. Spread this on the walls with a sponge or damp—not wet—towel. Let it set for a few minutes before wiping off stains and dirt. *(Keep in mind that wood finishes differ and this might not be the correct solution for your particular area. When in doubt, test a small area first.)*

- White rings or spots on wood furniture, if caused by heat sometimes respond to rubbing with a mixture of equal amounts of toothpaste and baking soda. Rub gently in a circular motion with a soft cloth. Apply furniture polish lightly, if necessary.

- Remove water spots from wooden floors by applying a baking soda solution on a damp rag. Remember wood should never be allowed to get really wet.

Surface Cleanups

- Use baking soda on a wet sponge to remove crayon stains from washable walls. Scrub gently. The combination will also take off most marks on the wall, including those from grease, pencil, and markers.

- Use a paste of baking soda and water to remove black scuff marks from linoleum floors.

- Safely remove crayon marks on a blackboard with the same paste.

- Remove some spilled inks from a linoleum floor by applying a dry paste to the stain and allowing it to sit a while before r e - moving and applying fresh powder to gently scrub it up.

Carpet Advice

- "Shampoo" your carpet with 1/2 cup baking soda mixed with 1 gallon warm water in a carpet cleaning machine or in a bucket, if you're scrubbing an area with a brush by hand. Sprinkle a very small amount of baking soda on specific stain areas on the dampened carpet, and let set a while before wiping the area with a sponge or clean towel. *(Test for colorfastness, first!)*

- Remove wine or grease stains from carpet by lightly sprinkling area immediately with baking soda. *(Table salt works, too—it's the sodium in sodium bicarbonate that is the magic element.)* Dab it up and add a little more if necessary. Leave on until the wine's been absorbed, then vacuum any residue that is left.

- Sap from Christmas trees can be cleaned from the carpet when "persuaded" with a paste of baking soda and water. Again, you'll need to vacuum up residue. *(Again, test for colorfastness.)*

- Dealing with vomit is tough enough; you don't want lingering odor or stain to remind you of the event. Prevent such after effects by cleaning up what you can, then generously sprinkling the remaining spot with baking soda. Scrub gently, from the outside toward the center with a stiff brush or sponge dipped repeatedly in clean water. Blot up the moisture with paper towels. Leave a last small layer of baking soda powder sprinkled on the spot and vacuum it later when the carpet is dry.

- Flush acid spills on carpeting (that's drain openers, toilet bowl cleaners and battery acid, as well as vomit and urine) with cool water immediately, if possible. Then neutralize with baking soda. You can worry about removing the baking soda residue from carpet after it's dry and your first aid efforts have worked.

- Sprinkle baking soda over carpets monthly, or as needed, before going to bed and let it set overnight. You may wish to use a stiff broom or brush to scrub it into the carpet. Vacuum the next day. Try this quick, sweet home maintenance plan. This home-made carpet deodorizer recipe calls for mixing:
  1/2 cup of baking soda
  1/2 cup cornstarch
  15 drops of your favorite essential oil fragrance

- Before the carpet layers put new carpeting down, sprinkle a box of baking soda over the floor—but not on hardwood floors— or the pad to be covered by the carpet. *(P.S. Don't let the carpet folks sweep it up before laying the carpet!)*

- Distribute baking soda evenly with a flour sifter, if you don't have a shaker.

- Fight flea problems with oil of rosemary, pennyroyal or citronella in place of your favorite fragrance. Sprinkle on carpet and just vacuum up.

- Create your signature fragrance throughout your home! Mix a box of baking soda with a few drops of your favorite potpourri oil or a little cinnamon or powdered cloves. Sprinkle on the carpet and vacuum.

- Add a small amount of baking soda to your vacuum bag to fight the dirty smell that vacuums can sometimes get.

  NOTE: Commercial carpet deodorizers are more granular and therefore easier to vacuum up than just regular baking soda.

Entree Ideas

- Sprinkle baking soda on indoor welcome mats to clean and deodorize, then vacuum. You use mats to catch dirt and grime—not spread it!

- Forget de-icing or rock salts, cat litter or sand! Just sprinkle baking soda on your front steps to provide traction and melt the ice. It won't damage outside surfaces, shoes or indoor surfaces if it is tracked inside. Mix with sand if you need greater texture.

- Scrub baking soda into outdoor mats with a broom and hose it down, or wait for the rains to do it for you.

Miscellaneous Maintenance

- Wash a cup of baking soda down a toilet or drain once a week to help maintain or restore the pH of a septic tank system. A favorable pH allows bacteria to break down and liquefy, which helps prevent clogging and backup in the tank and drain field. The regular addition of baking soda helps prevent corrosion of concrete as well as metal septic tanks, particularly the top of the tank, which is exposed to corrosive vapors.

- Make a paste of baking soda and water to fill nail holes in the wall and cracked plaster, as a temporary cover up. It dries and blends with white plaster. A more permanent solution calls for mixing the baking soda with household white glue.

- Clean smoke-blackened walls or ceilings with a damp rag and a strong solution of baking soda and water on a sponge or cloth.

- Clean upholstery by sprinkling it liberally with baking soda and letting it set for a few minutes before vacuuming. Smoke odors will also be eliminated.

- Use a baking soda paste to clean various types of vinyl.

- Baking soda provides a handy base for artificial flowers in an attractive container of your choosing that can be placed anywhere. Set alongside a litter box, and you have a decorative as well as deodorizing solution.

- Wash your waterbed mattress with a solution of baking soda and water if the plastic protector has a musty odor.

- Clean typewriter keys with a soft toothbrush and 4 tablespoons baking soda dissolved in 1 cup of water. Wipe with a tissue or paper towel.

- Clean dirty ivory—which yellows naturally with age, by the way—or plastic piano keys by rubbing with a soft cloth and a small amount of baking soda paste, being careful not to get it in between the keys. Buff with a dry cloth.

- Soak dirty mops and rags in a solution of 4 tablespoons baking soda to 1 quart water after washing dirt out, to get rid of residue smells. Rinse and let dry.

Hearth and Home

- Try placing a pie tin of baking soda in the fireplace to absorb lingering soot odors, after you've cleaned the ashes out.

- Keep a box of baking soda near the fireplace or wood burning stove to throw on a chimney fire, should one start. The soda will lower the temperature in the chimney and can help subdue, or even put out, the fire .

- Remove crayon marks from a fireplace hearth with equal parts vinegar and baking soda.

- Cleanup fireplace bricks with a mixture of baking soda and water.

Minimizing Musty Smells

- Fill old nylons with soda and suspend them from your basement ceiling to fight a damp and musty smell.

- Add 2 tablespoons baking soda to the water in your humidifier to eliminate musty smells.

- Keep musty odors out of seldom-used suitcases and trunks by sprinkling baking soda in them before they are stored.

- Sprinkle baking soda in toilets, down sink drains, in tubs and in showers before you go on vacation, to protect against stale odors.

- Remove a musty smell from blankets when you take them out of storage. Sprinkle them with baking soda and roll them up for a couple of hours. Then shake them out and fluff them in the dryer, without heat.

- Eliminate the residual musty smell after you've gotten rid of the water on wet carpeting by sprinkling a box of baking soda over it. Vacuum the next day.

- Leave open boxes of baking soda in your home workshop to remove paint and varnish smells.

- Smother—or at least reduce—stale cigarette odors by placing a little baking soda in the bottom of ashtrays.

- Get rid of the odor from plastic tablecloths by soaking them in a solution of water and baking soda.

Closet Fresheners

- Keep a small opened box of baking soda in closets, as you would your refrigerator, to absorb odors .

- Or mix equal amounts of baking soda and borax, which complement and enhance each other. Hide the mixture in a taped-up shoebox in which you've punched holes.

- Turn that musty closet smell into a sweet, fresh one by washing an uncarpeted floor with a mixture of 1/4 cup baking soda and 1/2 cup vinegar in 1 gallon warm water.

- Or just sprinkle baking soda on the closet floor—and in your shoes, too—on a weekly or monthly basis the day before you'll be vacuuming there.

  NOTE: Leather shoes can stiffen over time with the continual application of baking soda. Use accordingly. This does not affect canvas shoes, however.

- Place more than one open box of baking soda in an area where you want to remove the smell of mothballs.

- Toss a large homemade baking soda sachet in your clothes hamper, (see page 36) or sprinkle baking soda right in the hamper, to keep dirty clothes fresh-smelling until you're ready to wash them.

- Sprinkle a little soda in the bottom of a garment bag. Even it can benefit from baking soda.

Odor Eaters

- Place a "soda sachet" (see page 36) in sneakers so they don't smell up a closet. You might also mix some scented talcum with the baking soda.

- Sprinkle baking soda in shoes to neutralize smells. Those shoes with a "strong" personality would benefit from a liberal layer of baking soda, left overnight. In the morning, just tap the soda out. (*See note regarding leather shoes from previous page.*)

- Fight stinky shoes with baking soda in another way. Fill the toe sections from old socks or stockings with baking soda, and tie shut. Put these "soda ball's" in each shoe—and the odor should be history! And remember, dusting your feet first helps too!

CHAPTER SIX

LAUNDRY TIME

Baking soda will help you banish dirt, grime and unpleasant odors from soiled clothing and household linens. In short, it whitens, brightens and freshens.

Ideas For Your Clean Machine

- Add a 1/2 cup baking soda to the washing machine along with your usual amount of liquid laundry detergent for more effective cleaning. You'll have whiter socks and clothes and brighter colors. (*It doesn't boost powdered detergents, however.*)

- Flush acid spills on clothing, (acid drain openers, toilet bowl cleaners, battery acid, film developer, vomit and urine) with cool water immediately, then neutralize by sprinkling baking soda on them. If acid has dried on clothing, neutralize it with baking soda before putting it in the wash, or the water will reactivate the acid which will continue to damage the garment.

- Handle the mess when crayons accidentally left in a child's pocket have colored an entire wash load by rewashing the clothes in the hottest water allowable for the fabrics and adding 1/2 to 1 full box baking soda. Repeat if necessary.

- Add baking soda to wash water to remove age stains from linens and clothing. In addition, the baking soda softens the water, so you can use less detergent.

- Add 1/2 cup baking soda to your rinse cycle instead of fabric softener.

- Help remove stale mothball odors from clothes by adding 1/2 cup baking soda to the rinse water.

- Should your washer or dryer suffer the ravages of an accidental occurrence (such as gum left in a pocket), use a plastic scrubbie and a paste of baking to scrub the inside clean.

Brightness Boosters

- Boost your bleach's whitening power and save. When you might normally use 1 cup liquid chlorine bleach, if you add baking soda (1/2 cup to top loading machines, 1/4 cup to front loaders), you'll need only half that amount. Clothes get just as clean—with less bleach odor. And adding 1/4 to 1/2 cup baking soda to your regular amount of liquid chlorine bleach will get whites even whiter.

• Make a mild bleach for delicate fabrics with baking soda and lemon juice.

Stain Pre-Treatment

WARNING: Always test a small area of any fabric to determine colorfastness before any pre-treatment.

• Before laundering stained clothes, make a thick paste of 4 tablespoons or more baking soda and 1/4 cup warm water. Rub the paste on the spot and wash.

• Treat ring-around-the-collar by rubbing the same paste into the soiled area. Pour a little vinegar over this area just prior to washing.

• Make tar on clothing vanish by rubbing baking soda paste into the spot. Then wash the garment with baking soda instead of detergent.

• Remove yellow perfume stains by applying a paste of baking soda and ammonia *(be sure the garment is colorfast)*. Allow it to dry in the sun, if you can, then wash as usual.

• Remove perspiration stains and odor from washable fabrics by rubbing a paste of baking soda into the area before laundering. If stains are bad, allow paste to remain in place for two to three hours.

• Draw out blood stains on fabric by dampening them, then rubbing on baking soda. Follow this with a little hydrogen peroxide if it's safe for the fabric.

- Sprinkle baking soda on a fresh fruit or wine stain that has spilled on your table linens. Later—but as soon as possible—stretch the area tightly over a bowl or pan and pour boiling water over and through the baking soda. That should wash out the stain.

- Remove the acid smell of baby—or adult—spit-ups from clothes by rubbing dry baking soda on the spot. (Other laundry tips for children on page 72.)

The Nose Knows

- Remove the smell of smoke from clothes by soaking them in baking soda water before washing.

- Soak knit ski hats in baking soda and water to cut the sweaty odor before washing them.

- Remove gasoline and oil odors by placing clothes in a trash bag with baking soda for a few days before washing them.

- Deodorize work clothes that you can't wash right away. Sprinkle baking soda liberally into the pile of clothes. When they are ready to be washed, toss them in the machine as is.

- Presoak "skunked" clothes for several hours in water and baking soda (1/2 cup to 1 gallon water) before washing them, and you may not have to throw them out!

For Sensitive Souls

- To help remove chemical finishes on new clothes or fabrics, soak for two to six hours in water mixed with 1/2 to 2 cups vinegar. Rinse. Add 1/2 cup baking soda and run through the wash or soak up to two hours. Rinse again. (*WARNING: Vinegar may discolor some fabrics. Test a small area first.*)

- Use baking soda instead of fabric softener in the rinse cycle, if family members have sensitive skin.

- Rinse pool chlorine out of bathing suits in a sink full of water to which you've added 1 tablespoon baking soda.

Iron Ease
- Clean starch buildup or other residue from the bottom of a cool iron by rubbing it with a baking soda paste. Clean the steam holes with a cotton tip dipped in water, then baking soda. *(Yes, vinegar works well here, too.)*

Dry Cleaning
- Rub baking soda on a grease spot on polyester fabric. Brush off, and the stain should be gone.

- Remove crayon marks on fabric by rubbing very gently with baking soda sprinkled on a damp cloth.

- Remove ballpoint pen stain from leather clothing this way: Lay the item flat and spread baking soda on the stain. Leave it on until the ink is absorbed. Brush off. Repeat if necessary.

- Use a baking soda and water paste on a toothbrush or cloth to gently scrub grass stains from leather boots.

- Baking soda also acts as a suede cleaner. Rub it in with a soft brush, let it dry, and brush off.

For Shoe
- Before polishing shoes, remove black scuff marks with a paste of baking soda and water. Leather won't be damaged, and you'll have a clean shoe to shine.

- If knotted shoelaces or cords are getting you tied in knots, sprinkle on a little baking soda. Knots will pull out more easily.

- Sprinkle baking soda inside smelly shoes after wearing them. Shake out excess powder the next morning in the sink or toilet bowl. It will significantly reduce shoe odor and closet odors.

Sweet Sweats

- Sprinkle 1/2 cup baking soda in a gym bag at night. Vacuum out soda and odors in the morning.

- Keep an open or vented box in your gym locker. A vented box will also travel easily in your gym bag.

- Sprinkle baking soda into clean socks before you put them on for the ultimate in controlling foot smell and moisture.

- Add a little baking soda to your street shoes when changing to workout clothes or swim suit at the health club. It will be more pleasant to put them in your locker and on your feet when you get dressed to leave.

Personal Accents Cleanups

- Revive tarnished silver pieces with the same solution (using aluminium and hot water with baking soda on page 35) but also remember not all sources recommend this as a good polishing procedure. You might not want to use it on heirlooms or very special items.

- Make an excellent cleaner for jewelry, including silver pieces, from a paste of baking soda and mild dish soap or shampoo. Apply with a dry cloth or an old toothbrush to clean tiny crannies.

- Fizz away grime from gold jewelry by covering the pieces with baking soda, then pouring vinegar over it. Rinse clean. *(Don't soak items with gemstones or faux pearls, however.)* This can also work well on costume jewelry pieces that can handle soaking in water.

- For a quick jewelry touch up, rub a bit of paste of baking soda onto the jewelry, rinse it off and buff dry.

- Rub a pinch of baking soda on dulled pearls to restore their original shine. Wipe clean with a damp, very soft cloth.

- Restore the tarnished silver and clouded crystal beads of old rosaries by soaking them for five to ten minutes in baking soda and water. Gently brush them and rinse clean.

- Cleanse and "program" natural crystals in baking soda, some say.

CHAPTER SEVEN

HYGIENE & GROOMING

Baking soda belongs with your grooming aids as well as with your cleaning equipment. It has special uses for hair and skin care, for dental health, and even for eyes and ears!

Hair

- Remove buildup on your hair from concentrated shampoos and hair sprays by mixing 1 teaspoon baking soda in your hand with your shampoo and lathering as usual. Condition, too, as continual use alone could be drying to your hair.

- If pool chlorine is turning your blond hair green, get in the habit of rinsing your hair after swimming with a solution of 1/2 cup baking soda dissolved in lemon juice. This mixture bubbles up and should be poured over your hair promptly, after you've wet your hair.

- Drop combs and brushes in the sink to soak in a solution of hot water and 1/4 cup baking soda. Watch the dirt fizz away.

- Brush baking soda into your hair to whiten it for a play or costume party. As a plus, it will give your hair added shine when you wash it out.

Skin Solutions

- Avoid allergic reactions to bubble baths and still pamper your self at bath time by mixing 1 cup baking soda and 1/4-1/2 cup baby oil in the bath water. It softens skin and helps avoid winter dry-skin itchies. Please be careful as tub may become slippery.

- Cool down on hot days with a tepid shower. If you have heat rash, wash with a soapless cleanser such as Dove and, after patting yourself dry, dab a paste of baking soda on any rash areas and let it remain on as long as is feasible.

- Be aware that a sunburn can be soothed by soaking in lukewarm bath water to which you've added a generous amount— from a half to a whole box of baking soda.

- Try a dry baking soda paste or baking soda mixed with your facial cleanser to make a good, mild facial scrub.

- Or make a facial scrub by mixing 1 teaspoon each baking soda and olive oil to form a slightly thicker paste. Massage it gently into your skin and rinse well before patting dry.

- Try a watery paste of baking soda instead of shaving cream or soap lather when shaving. For razor burns, dab on a solution of baking soda and water for temporary relief.

- Blitz zits with a thick paste of baking soda and peroxide applied before bedtime.

Deodorant Action

- Baking soda can be sprinkled (see page 36 for shaker ideas) or patted on as a deodorant. It contains no other chemicals so is comfortable to use even right after shaving under your arms.

- Mix a little baking soda with a little talcum for a smoother-textured powder.

- Dust baking soda lightly over inner thighs and genital areas to act as a safe deodorant and moisture absorber.

- Sprinkle a dusting's worth of baking soda over a sanitary pad before using for extra deodorizing protection.

- When there's no time to shower, rinse a sponge or wash cloth in a sink half filled with water and several tablespoons baking soda. Squeeze out excess water and wipe yourself down, for a good freshener.

Hand Care

- Keep hands soft by sprinkling baking soda in dish water when washing the dishes.

- Use baking soda to clean marker stains off your hands.

- Clean nails with a dab of baking soda on a small nail brush. Scrub gently under exposed nail area too. Dirt dissolves and rinses away—especially garden dirt.

- Keep cuticles smooth by slightly moistening baking soda and rubbing it in around nails. Rinse off and wipe hands dry.

- Use a paste of baking soda to smooth away rough skin on elbows.

Eye and Visionwear Care
- Relieve itchy eyes from allergies or make-up residue. Splash a solution of baking soda and warm water in the eyes—unless you're sensitive to saline—*salt*—solutions.

- Make a paste of contact lens solution and baking soda to gently rub clean soft contact lenses—but not gas perms. Clean gently with your fingers. Rinse lenses thoroughly with saline solution. This treatment—used infreqently—reduces protein buildup on the lenses.

- Sprinkle some baking soda on dirty eyeglasses over a sink. With wet fingers, rub the baking soda gently over the lenses of your glasses. Rinse the glasses clean under tap water and dry with a lint-free cloth.

Breath Freshener
- Sprinkle about 1/2 teaspoon baking soda, in a cup of water and rinse your mouth as you would with any mouthwash. It will remove onion or garlic scents as well as morning mouth, and leave you with a fresh—as opposed to artificial—taste in your mouth. By changing the pH balance in your mouth, it makes it a less friendly environment for many bacteria.

• Make your own mouthwash/breath freshener by combining:
> 1 teaspoon salt
> 1 teaspoon baking soda
> 1 quart water

Dental Home Hygiene

• Dip a damp toothbrush in a little baking soda sprinkled into the palm of your hand. Brush as usual. Use your hand to rinse clean the skin, taking advantage of the baking soda "remnants."

• Make your own toothpaste by combining:
> 3 tablespoons baking soda
> 1 tablespoon popcorn salt *(because of its finer grain)*
> 1-1/2 tablespoons glycerin *(from a pharmacy)*
> 10 -12 drops flavoring *(peppermint, cinnamon, etc.)*
> 1-2 drops water

(Baking soda has been used for decades as a home dentifrice. It is less abrasive than most toothpastes yet is still strong enough to clean effectively. But it doesn't contain fluoride—a chemical recommended to help prevent cavities in pre-adult teeth.)

• Or just add a little artificial sugar substitute to a container of baking soda for a simple, more pleasant tasting tooth cleanser.

• Or add enough flavored fluoride mouth wash to make a paste of baking soda and store it in a small, covered jar.

• Since hydrogen peroxide is said to be an excellent aid in fighting gingivitis, mix these ingredients together in a glass container for a paste:
> 2 tablespoons baking soda
> 1 tablespoons hydrogen peroxide
> 1/2 teaspoon mint extract (optional)

Hydrogen peroxide has a short shelf life in a mixture, so use it promptly.

- Dab or gently apply a paste of baking soda to sore gums. Brush regularly with a homemade paste of baking soda when caring for the early stages of gum disease.

- Dip dental floss in baking soda before flossing, and you'll be removing plaque while you floss.

- Add 1 teaspoon baking soda to your dental Waterpik. This leaves your mouth feeling clean and tasting great. Those with braces will especially appreciate the feeling.

- And brushing braces with baking soda alone will make them REALLY shine!

- Soak toothbrushes in baking soda and warm water overnight for sparkling clean bristles.

- Get relief from canker sores by neutralizing the acids in your mouth. Swish with some baking soda in a glass of water. Or put a small amount of it in paste-form on the area with your finger. Hold it there as long as is feasible, then rinse with plain water.

Keep Your Pearly Whites Looking That Way

- For an occasional whitener treatment, mix together:
        1 teaspoon baking soda
        1/2 teaspoon lemon juice

Apply a coat of this paste to your teeth, using a cotton swab. Brush clean with water, then rinse. Coffee and tea stains will disappear.

   WARNING: *Lemon juice is a strong acid and if used alone can damage tooth enamel. The buffering effect of baking soda prevents this. Lemon juice should not be used regularly in any cleaning solution for teeth.*

- For another whitener, mix:
  >   1 part toothpaste
  >   1 part baking soda
  >   1 part hydrogen peroxide

  Brush with this once a week to remove stains on teeth. Do not swallow!

Denture Soak

- To sweeten and clean dentures, soak them in a cup for 30 minutes in a mixture of:
  >   1 tablespoon baking soda
  >   1 tablespoon powdered Tide detergent
  >   1 cup water

  Rinse well before using

- Or simply soak dentures in a glass or cup of water with 2 teaspoons baking soda.

- Use the above solution for cleaning plastic retainers, too.

Ears

- Dislodge ear wax—and prevent wax buildup—with a mixture of baking soda and water. Put into ears with an eye dropper.

Feet

- Soothe aching feet in a solution of 4 tablespoons baking soda and 1 quart hot water to dissipate odors and bring comfort to your tender toes.

- Try regular foot baths in baking soda to control persistent foot odor.

- Beautify those toe tappers by soaking them in a softening solution of warm water and baking soda before using a pumice stone to remove calluses, ground-in dirt and dead skin.

• Try using baking soda in place of expensive foot powders to control athlete's foot, some say. Sprinkle it on dry or make a paste to rub between your toes. Rinse the paste off after 15 minutes and dry feet thoroughly. Also dust shoes and socks with baking soda before wearing them. Baking soda reduces foot moisture, which makes a fertile area for any foot fungus.

CHAPTER EIGHT

HOME REMEDIES

For easing and soothing many minor complaints, baking soda's unbeatable. Check with your doctor before using it medicinally, but once you get the go-ahead, you'll find it invaluable.

As an Antacid

Read the following before ingesting baking soda:

Though it is long known for its antacid qualities for relieving what is commonly referred to as heartburn or acid indigestion, it is important not to turn this use for baking soda into an inappropriate home remedy when consulting with a physician would be the appropriate action. The manufacturers of baking soda warn that one should also NOT ingest any antacids when the stomach is overly full to avoid possible injury to the stomach. It is also NOT a remedy for other types of stomach complaints such as nausea, stomach aches, cramps, gas pains, peptic ulcers or stomach distention caused by over-eating and/or over-drinking. Do not take baking soda without a doctor's okay if you're on a restricted sodium diet. Patients on heart medications are frequently warned not to use standard antacids. A small amount of baking soda stirred in water is sometimes recommended as a safe alternative. Check with your doctor first. Pregnant women should consult their doctor as well. And lastly, do not use this maximum dosage for more than two consecutive weeks.

WARNING
Too much antacid can cause over-alkalinity problems which might endanger your health. It's important to follow given guidelines for usage.

- Alleviate acid indigestion using the follow suggested dosage:
     1/2 level teaspoon baking soda
     1/2 glass of water

  Wait 2 hours before taking an additional dosage. Maximum dosage per person up to 60 years of age would be eight 1/2 teaspoons in a 24 hour period.

- If you dislike the taste of baking soda but love the relief, empty inexpensive vitamin capsules and refill them with baking soda. Drink a glass or two of water with each capsule, following dosage recommendations above.

- Make an effervescent antacid by mixing in a glass:
                1 tablespoon vinegar
                1/2 teaspoon sugar
                1/2 cup water
                1/2 teaspoon baking soda
  Drink immediately while it's fizzing. (*Alka-Seltzer is a commercial remedy that contains sodium bicarbonate and aspirin.*)

- If aspirin gives you indigestion, add 1/2 teaspoon baking soda to the glass of water with which you swallow one.

Bladder Home Remedies

- Treat or relieve bladder infections, say some, by drinking baking soda in water every two hours for two or three days, on the assumption that you can chemically alter your body's pH balance. (*Should you choose to try this be sure to follow dosage recommendations on the previous page.*)

- Baking soda in the bath can bring relief from the burning sensations and skin inflammation that accompany urinary infections.

- Douche twice a day with 2 tablespoons baking soda to 1 quart warm water to relieve vaginal itching common to menstrual onset. Soaking in such a solution may relieve vaginitis or anal itching as well.

Mineral Replacement Drink

- Create an inexpensive drink which replaces salts lost from such problems as diarrhea or vomiting—often know as the "GI drink"— as follows: for each quart of boiled water, add 1 level teaspoon table salt, 1 rounded teaspoon baking soda, and 4 rounded teaspoons sugar. Stir until clear and add 1 package of sugarless Kool-Aid or similar flavoring drink product. Make it fresh daily and keep it in the refrigerator.

Stop Smoking
• Baking soda may help you stop smoking, say researchers at the Mayo Clinic. If you're not on a low-sodium diet, when nicotine withdrawal begins, you may get short term relief by drinking a mixture of 2 teaspoons baking soda in a glass of water. The bubbly water relieves the urge to smoke. *(This is not recommended on a repetitive basis and guidelines for ingesting baking soda on page 67 should be noted.)*

Sore Throat
• Melt 1 aspirin in 2 teaspoons hot water. Add a level teaspoon baking soda and an additional 1/2 cup hot water and mix gently. Gargle to ease sore throat pain. Repeat as needed.

• Mix equal parts baking soda, brown sugar and salt in a glass of warm water and gargle.

Stuffy Nose
• Clear adult nasal passages with a mixture of 1/4 teaspoon baking soda and 1 tablespoon water. Place a drop or two in each nostril and very shortly you will feel relief from a stuffy nose.

• Add a teaspoon of baking soda to your vaporizer to help with chest congestion—unless your vaporizer directions indicate that additives can't be used—and helps keep the unit clean at the same time.

Bee Stings—Bug Bites
• Make a paste of baking soda and pat it on bee stings and other itchy insect bites for immediate RELIEF. Leave on to dry. Repeat with a new paste, if necessary. *(Stings can also be treated with meat tenderizer sprinkled on a wet cloth or gauze bandage. Follow up with a baking soda soak.)* P.S. Diluted vinegar is suggested for wasp stings.

- Soak in a warm bath with 1/2 cup of baking soda to help soothe rashes from chicken pox or poison ivy, or apply baking soda with wet compresses.

Burns
- Treat acid spills on the skin (those from such products as acid drain openers, toilet bowl cleaners, battery acid, and film developer) immediately. Flush the area with cool water at once and neutralize by sprinkling baking soda on the affected part.

- Treat burns by quickly applying cold cloths dipped in ice water with baking soda added until the burn has no heat. The burn is less likely to blister with this treatment. *(Some hospital emergency rooms are said to do this.)*

Other Skin Problems
- Cope with sunburn discomfort by mixing 1/4 cup of baking soda with 1/2 cup of cornstarch in a tub of tepid water and soak as long and as often as you can manage.

- Relieve pain of blisters from shingles or other rashes by applying handfuls of baking soda to the blisters, making a paste, while bathing in tepid water.

- Soothe itching caused by dry skin or psoriasis by using a weak solution of baking soda—1/3 cup to 1 gallon water. Apply to the area with a washcloth.

- Clean out dirt from narrow cuts, such as paper cuts or dirty splinter punctures, with a paste of baking soda. Rinse and repeat until the area is clean.

- Sprinkle baking soda very lightly on and inside a cast to eliminate odor. Blow it "in" using a hair dryer.

CHAPTER NINE

LITTLE TYKES

Baking soda is unexcelled for baby complaints, top to bottom.
And it's as helpful in the nursery, playroom and backyard as it is
in every other area of living space.

New Baby Tips

• Keep baby bottles, nipples, and rims fresh by soaking overnight in a large bowl filled with hot water and 1/2 box baking soda. Or boil the bottles for three minutes in 3 tablespoons baking soda and water.

• Sprinkle a cup of baking soda on the bottom of the diaper pail before putting in the plastic liner, or sprinkle some in the disposable diaper pail before, after or during its use to control odors. Its deodorant effect is wonderfully effective.

• Keep a small squeeze bottle filled with a solution of half water and half baking soda. When baby spits up, neutralize the spot with a squirt and blot.

• When your baby upchucks on your shirt wipe up excess, then sprinkle the spot with baking soda. Let it dry and brush it off. Odor is gone and the stain doesn't set. Carry a small container of baking soda in your diaper bag or purse for such emergencies.

• Wash new baby clothes to remove any chemical finishes by washing them in mild soap and 1/2 cup baking soda.

Coping with Cradle Cap

• Conquer cradle cap with a paste of baking soda and water. Leave it on the baby's head for a few moments before bath time, then rinse the scalp clean. *(The same paste also removes sand — from the beach or the sandbox—from a toddler's scalp.)*

• Or try this method: Apply baby oil to the scalp, then rub baking soda into the oily hair. Comb the baby's hair and scalp gently, loosening flaky skin. Shampoo and rinse clean.

• Or mix 1 tablespoon baking soda with 4 tablespoons petroleum jelly and rub on the infant's scalp. Wash out after leaving it on for ten or fifteen minutes.

- Clean your baby's combs and brushes in a basin of warm water and 1 teaspoon baking soda. Swish, soak, rinse and dry before using.

Better Bottoms

- Fight diaper rash by sprinkling a little baking soda in warm water—NOT alone as a powder—for cleaning baby's bottom areas. The baking soda soothes and helps diaper rash heal by neutralizing the acid from urine.

- Soak soiled cloth diapers waiting to be washed in this solution:
      1/2 cup baking soda
      2 quarts warm water

- Add 1/2 cup baking soda to your baby's bathwater to help relieve diaper rash. Use a smaller amount if you are bathing baby in a sink or a plastic baby tub.

Mother's Medicine

- Lower a feverish baby's temperature by putting him or her in a bath of lukewarm water to which you've added some baking soda.

- Treat infants' aphthae _(little white patches in the mouth)_ or red, cracking skin in the corner of the mouth by sponging the mouth with a sterile gauze pad soaked in warm water and baking soda. Apply four or five times a day.

- Treat an infant's or young child's stuffy nose with a mixture of 1/4 teaspoon baking soda and 1/2 teaspoon salt added to 1 cup boiled water. Let the mixture cool before putting it in a clean bottle with an eye dropper (available at the drug store) to use as a nose dropper. Administer only a drop or two at a time. Check time intervals with your doctor.

Kids' Stuff

- Clean bassinets, changing tables, crib railings, car seat, and such, safely with baking soda and water.

- Get rid of spaghetti, catsup or crayon stains on a plastic high chair tray by sprinkling the tray with baking soda. Rub with a damp cloth, then rinse clean.

- Return babies' white shoes to their original luster by cleaning and polishing them with baking soda on a damp wash cloth.

- Let preschoolers join the fun of chores by using baking soda as a safe nontoxic "scrubbing cleanser" to clean the tub.

- Freshen your children's dolls by cleaning them with a paste of dishwasher detergent and baking soda. The combination removes stains—including ink! Get tiny crevices clean by dipping an old toothbrush or cotton swab in baking soda.

- Clean a stuffed animal or fabric toy that can't be washed, by shaking it in a bag with baking soda which will absorb the dirt and grime. Let it sit for 15 minutes before brushing, shaking and/or vacuuming the dry baking soda off.

- Clean and deodorize kids' toy chests and toys by wiping them clean with a baking soda solution applied with a damp cloth or a sponge.

- Brush a paste of baking soda and water on the contact points of old toys or flashlights to clean battery corrosion and renew connections.

- Clean a child's bicycle helmet with baking soda to leave the finish shiny.

Mother's Magic

- Keep a box of baking soda near your dryer. Sprinkle it in your children's pajama sleeper feet after drying to help avoid future smelly feet.

- Use baking soda when children wet the bed at night. Remove bed linens and spread baking soda over the wet area of the mattress. Let it soak up the moisture and the odor. When dry, vacuum up the soda. Throw additional baking soda into the laundry with the wet bed clothes to neutralize the urine smell.

- Before storing children's plastic pool and inflatable toys, dry everything thoroughly, then sprinkle evenly with baking soda before rolling them up for storage. This treatment eliminates the threat of mildew, hoses off easily in the spring and leaves everything clean for the new season.

- Send a box of baking soda to school several times a year with a youngster who's willing to freshen his or her smelly gym locker with one. Just let your child know that all that is required is to place it at the back of the locker with the top off or open, or with holes punched in the top.

CHAPTER TEN

PLAY PROJECTS FOR KIDS

Just reach for your box of baking soda the next time the kids say, "Gee, there's nothing to do." Of course there's something to do, if you have baking soda on hand. Try these favorites with your children and they'll call you *Merlin Mom, the Magnificent.*

Stencil Carpet Fun
- Create a family tradition of carpet prints to mark the holidays. Make or buy stencils that you sprinkle baking soda on to create white powder prints. These clean up easily with a vacuum.
  - Δ Bunny footprints to lead your children to their Easter baskets
  - Δ Santa footprints from the fireplace or the front door.
  - Δ Turkey feet at Thanksgiving
  - Δ Heart shapes at Valentine's Day

- Use stencil letters to spell out names or happy holiday messages with baking soda or just to let little ones practice learning their letters and numbers.

- Make a WELCOME HOME stencil to use on your entry carpet—or front stoop—to greet returning loved ones.

Arts & Crafts Ideas
- Make or buy stencils to create nontoxic designs on windows, paper, and cards with a baking soda-and-water paste, with food color added. Apply the paste with a sponge.

- Rub off crayon marks on a blackboard with a paste of baking soda and water. This method doesn't scratch the board. (*The same technique works well on most house surfaces unexpectedly decorated with crayons and even some markers.*)

- Mix a small amount of baking soda into children's tempera paints to make cleanup easier. It also keeps paints fresher and smoother.

Volcanic Action
- Let kids play "chemist" safely by mixing baking soda and vinegar and watch it boil and fizz in different containers.

- If you want an interesting comparison, put 1/2 cup hot vinegar in one cup and 1/2 cup vinegar that has been chilled with ice cubes in another. Drop a teaspoon of baking soda into each cup and watch the differing reaction times.

- Fill a small coffee cup, custard cup or empty yogurt container one-third to half full of vinegar. Cut a 4-inch square piece of tissue or paper towel and place 1 teaspoon baking soda in it. Pull the four corners together and twist the "package" shut. Drop it into the vinegar and watch the reaction!
  HINT: The hotter the vinegar, the faster reaction you will get. In fact fill one container with hot vinegar and one with cold vinegar to see the different reacting times. The explanation is that particles move faster at higher temperature.

- To create a "volcano mountain," turn a flower pot upside down in a low, broad pan (which will catch the "volcanic" spill over). On the flower pot, put an empty tuna can over which a small paper or plastic cup has been set, also upside down. Tape the tuna can well at its circular seam to the cup now resting on it. Cover all three together with aluminum foil to create a silver mountain or volcanic shape. Make a hole at the top of this "mountain"—the top is actually the bottom of the paper cup— and add several spoonfuls of baking soda and a bit of dishwashing detergent. Next add some red food coloring to 1/2 cup vinegar and pour it through the top hole and watch the eruption begin!

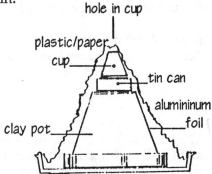

hole in cup

plastic/paper cup

tin can

alumininum foil

clay pot

A DO-IT-YOURSELF VOLCANO KIT

You can purchase a safe, ready-made kit that includes soft moldable clay, a plastic vial, a tray and instructions. You just add the baking soda and vinegar! It *(item #3038775)* is available for $12.95 plus p/h from: Edmund Scientific Company, 60 Pearce Ave, Tonawanda, NY 14150. Call them at (800) 728-6999. Or for a few dollars more, you can buy their deluxe kit called the Smithsonian Erupting Volcano Kit *(item #3052367).* www.scientifsonline.com

• Add some excitement to your child's sandbox by creating a "volcanic eruption." Set a juice glass filled with vinegar in a sand-made "mountain." Add 1 tablespoon baking soda and watch the action.

"Bouncing Balls" in a Bowl

Amuse your kids by combining in a clear glass container the following:

> water—filling the container
> *(optional: add food coloring for drama)*
> 1/4 cup vinegar
> 3 teaspoons baking soda

Add light weight items such as buttons or small uncooked pasta pieces and watch them "bounce!" *(Mothballs work well here, but don't use them if you have a child young enough to put one in his or her mouth.)*

Though the items will sink at first, they will begin to rise because the bubbles created by the vinegar and baking soda reaction cling to them, lifting them to the surface. At the surface the air bubbles break and they fall back to the bottom and the 5process begins again. Renew the solution with 3 parts vinegar to 1 part baking soda as needed. *(HINT: Powdered citric acid or lemon juice concentrate can be used in place of vinegar.)*

Inflatables

Make a magical inflating balloon. First, put 2 teaspoons baking soda into an empty soda bottle with a funnel. Clean the funnel and use it to pour 1/3 cup vinegar into the balloon. Carefully stretch the neck of a balloon over the mouth of the bottle and pull it down 3/4 inch while the liquid in the balloon hangs to one side. While holding the neck of the balloon around the neck of the bottle, lift up the balloon to empty the vinegar into the bottle. The reaction between it and the baking soda will cause fizzing and produce carbon dioxide gas which will inflate the balloon. The balloon will also feel warm from the heat/energy produced by the chemical reaction.

Classic Craft Clay—Stove Top Method

Cook and stir over medium heat the following, until thickened:

        2 cups (1 lb. box) baking soda
        1 cup corn starch
        1-1/4 cups cold water—with food coloring added

When the mixture feels like moist mashed potatoes (approximately 10 to 15 minutes), spread it on a plate or sheet of foil and cover it with a damp cloth until it's cool enough to handle. Knead or pat for a couple of minutes until smooth. Add food coloring here, if you have not done so before. Store it—or any unused portions of it—in the refrigerator in a plastic bag or air-tight container until you use it. It's good for up to a week.
HINT: If you don't want the temporary tint of food coloring on your hands, wear disposable plastic gloves.

Mold into shapes that are not too thick, or they won't dry well. Or roll out on waxed paper and use cookie cutters for shapes to decorate. If you're making hanging ornaments, use a straw to punch out a hanging hole.

In a shallow foil dish or pan, place some of the clay about an inch thick and let your child push down into it with one hand—

fingers spread—to make an impression. When it has hardened, write the name, age and date on the back of this memento with a marker.

Clay items take 1-2 days to air dry (depending on thickness) or can be baked for 10-15 minutes in the oven on the lowest setting. Turn occasionally to dry both sides well. Or you can preheat your oven to 350°F. Turn the oven off and place finished items on a cookie sheet in the oven. Leave there until the oven is cold. You can even use your microwave oven if you do just a few pieces at a time on a paper towel for 30 seconds a side. Continue to turn items every 30 seconds until they feel dry to the touch.

Paint cooled, hardened pieces with poster paints, water colors or acrylics. Apply glitter to wet paint. Use a waterproof marker for adding finer details. Pieces can be protected with a layer of shellac, acrylic varnish or just use clear nail polish.

OTHER ITEMS TO MAKE:
Shapes using cookie cutters; beads from oval to elongated shapes (make a hole using a toothpick while the clay is still moist); hand print plaques; small picture frames; items you can add magnets to the back of; holiday decorations, including Christmas tree ornaments; or a carved sculpture from a dried "block" of craft clay.

Playdough—Microwave-Made

Mix dry ingredients:	Mix wet ingredients:
2 cups flour	2 cups water
1 cup salt	1 tablespoon cooking oil
1/2 cup cornstarch	dash of food coloring
1 tablespoon baking soda	

Combine mixtures in a large glass bowl. Microwave on HIGH for 3 or 4 minutes, stirring after each minute. Knead on countertop and store in plastic container. Create different textures by adding sand, oatmeal, or even sawdust to the dough.

Edible Cookie Sculpture Dough
Mix the dry ingredients:

        5-1/2 cups flour
        3 teaspoons baking soda
        1/4 teaspoon salt

Mix wet ingredients until the sugar is dissolved:

        1 cup shortening
        2 cups sugar
        1/2 cup boiling water
        1 teaspoon vanilla
        1 teaspoon lemon juice

Combine the two. The dough will have a nice consistency. Refrigerate up to 3 days (or freeze) what you will not be using that day, but remember that the dough will need to reach room temperature before you can shape it when you take it out.

Use the dough to make free form sculptures *(not TOO thick)* or roll out the dough about 1/4 inch thick and use cookie cutters or make free-form designs yourself. Place your hand down on the dough and use a plastic knife to cut away at the outline of your hand. Or insert wooden popsicle sticks horizontally in the dough to make Cookie Pops. Make "appliques" on the larger piece with small pieces of dough cut in dots, small ropes, little triangles, or other shapes.

Brush the finished sculptures with a beaten egg before baking if you'd like them to have a nice, golden shine.

Bake at 300°F for 20 to 30 minutes or until golden. Let them cool for 5 to 10 minutes before removing from the cookie sheet. Display *and/or* eat!

CHAPTER ELEVEN

Humane Animal Treatment

If the pets ain't comfortable, ain't nobody comfortable, to para-phrase a familiar saying. You're not comfortable if they're not clean and odor-free, either. Baking soda can help you in both areas.

Pet Peeves

- After cleaning up a pet stain, liberally sprinkle with baking soda and let set overnight before vacuuming. Odors will disappear. (*CAUTION: While sprinkling baking soda on a wet area can be an effective cleaner and deodorizer on carpet or upholstery, not all fabrics are color fast. Always test a small, hidden area first.*)

- Clean pet urine on carpets by making a paste of water and baking soda. Put over stain and let set until dry. Then vacuum. (See additional carpet cleaning ideas on page 44.)

- Wash the insides of animals ears with a solution of warm water and baking soda to eliminate itching and ear mites.

- Soak and squeeze a sponge in a warm water and baking soda solution. Rub the sponge gently over your cat's coat to remove loose hairs, thus preventing hair balls.

- If you keep pet food dishes outside, sprinkle baking soda around them. This usually deters insects from approaching the dish and won't harm your animal.

Kitty Poos

- Before adding litter to any freshly started cat box, sprinkle a layer of baking soda first.

- Keep your cat's litter box fresh and odorless inexpensively. Use generic clay litter and sprinkle baking soda generously with each change.

- Add to scoopable cat litter as needed to control odors.

- Recycle newspapers and save money at the same time. Shred or rip newspapers and mix pieces with baking soda. Discard frequently!

Canine Come-Clean Ideas

- Scrub dog collars with a solution of baking soda dissolved in hot water to remove grease and grime. Or soak nylon collars in a solution of equal parts baking soda and vinegar in hot water. The collar will soak clean in 15 minutes to a half hour. Rinse and hang up to dry.

- Sprinkle a small amount of baking soda on your dog and brush out to remove doggy odor.

- Add 2 tablespoons baking soda to your dog's bath water and to the rinse water for a soft and shiny coat.

- If your white dog gets dirty, clean it with baking soda sprinkled right on the coat. Brush out the dirt.

- Has Rover been sprayed by the neighborhood skunk? Bathe him in a tub of water to which you add 1 box baking soda, the juice of 2 lemons and a squeeze of your shampoo.

- Add 1/2 cup baking soda to wash water when washing pet blankets to help clean and deodorize.

- Brush dogs' teeth with a solution of baking soda and water with a toothbrush—if they will let you. It will certainly clean and freshen their breath. (*NOTE: Not all vets feel baking soda is a good toothpaste for dogs and cats because of its sodium content.*)

Pooch Puddles

- While housebreaking puppies, use baking soda on the urine spots to make sure the odor is gone or they'll want to reuse the same spot again.

- Sprinkle baking soda on pet stains even on concrete. It will soak up the moisture—and the odor.

• Sprinkle baking soda lightly under frequently used trees to counter act the acid of pet urine. It will, however, kill any grass that is there.

Dog Ditties

• Clean your dog's toys safely using baking soda. For plastic toys, mix a solution and wash. Give stuffed or furry toys a "dry shower" by sprinkling on baking soda and allowing it to sit for 15 minutes before brushing off.

• Ease, and cool a dog's skin eruptions with soaking in water to which you've added baking soda.

• Make a pillow for your dog. Fill it with poly-fiberfill and sprinkle baking soda inside before you sew it closed. The soda keeps the dog—as well as the pillow— smelling fresh.

• Freshen your dog's bedding by sprinkling on dry baking soda and letting it set at least 15 minutes before vacuuming it up.

Other Pet Problems

• Cover the bottom of the hamster cage with baking soda to control odors then cover with wood shavings.

• Deodorize bird, guinea pig, and rabbit cages by sprinkling baking soda underneath their newspaper liner too. It's harmless to your pets.

• When spring cleaning your pet bird's abode, use a solution of baking soda instead of detergent to do the job.

• Clean aquarium-type cages you use for hamsters or mice with baking soda. If your kitchen sink isn't large enough to hold it, put the aquarium in the bath or shower. Fill it with water and

1/2 cup baking soda and it will easily scrub clean.

- Soak plastic bird feeders in a solution of hot water and baking soda to avoid cleaning solution odor.

- Lower dangerously high acid levels in aquariums—and raise the pH if testing requires it—by using 1/4 teaspoon baking soda to 10 gallons of water.

- Keep horses' legs clean by washing them with a solution of baking soda and water.

CHAPTER TWELVE

HANDY DANDY IDEAS

Real men don't use baking soda—NOT! Indoor and outdoor projects benefit from its cleaning, neutralizing and odor eliminating properties, be they in the capable hands of men or women.

Outdoor Dos

- Scrub a wooden deck with a mixture of 2 cups baking soda to 1 gallon water, for a weathered look. This solution may, however, affect stains or finishes so test a small area first.

- Treat oil stains (baby oil, suntan lotion and such) on wood decks by sprinkling baking soda liberally on the area. Let it set for an hour or so before sweeping it away. Absorbing the stain may turn the baking soda yellow. Repeat if necessary. Or wet the stain area with a bit of paint thinner and immediately sprinkle baking soda on the wet area to prevent the thinner from soaking into the wood.

- Wipe down lawn furniture—especially pieces with plastic webbing—with a solution of baking soda and water before putting it away for the winter. Sprinkle it directly on canvas chairs, hammocks and the like. Shake off excess and store.

- Remove tape residue left on windows and woodwork after you've taken down plastic insulation in the spring, with a baking soda paste.

- Remove playdough from cement by applying equal amounts of baking soda and water to the area. Scrub with a stiff brush until playdough is removed.

- Pour some baking soda into your garden hose, replace the nozzle and turn the water on. Then spray to wash the grime off white aluminum siding.

Workshop/Garage

- Cleaning oil-based paint from brushes and tools requires using paint thinner. But how do you clean the thinner off the brushes? Soak everything in warm water and baking soda.

- Rejuvenate stiff and hardened paint brushes by boiling them in a solution of:
  >1/2 gallon water
  >1 cup baking soda
  >1/4 cup vinegar

- Keep a solution of 1/2 cup baking soda and 1/2 cup water in a container in your workshop to neutralize accidental acid spills or sprays that may come working with batteries and the like.

- Immediately sprinkle baking soda right from the box if an acid has come in contact with any part of the body. Rinse area with water and repeat treatment.

- Keep carpenter ants, silver fish and roaches from invading by laying down a barrier of baking soda under sink-pipe openings and along basement windows. Roaches eat the baking soda, dehydrate, then die. *(This "pesticide" is nontoxic to children and pets.)*

- Clean oil from the garage floor by pouring a little paint thinner on the oil area and covering it with baking soda. Let it set overnight. Sweep up the baking soda and dispose of it. Or use the baking soda alone to soak up the oil.

Assault Your Battery

- Neutralize battery corrosion (that white powdery buildup) on posts and cables by applying a paste of baking soda to the area. Wipe or brush terminals clean and apply petroleum jelly to prevent future corrosion.

- Be environmentally responsible. Neutralize the acid in old car batteries when they are no longer in use. Mix a solution of equal parts baking soda and water, and fill each battery cell.

- Unclog a radiator by draining the radiator and refilling it with water and a one-pound box of baking soda. Run the car for a few minutes, then drain and fill with antifreeze. This is NOT recommended for cars with aluminium block engines, however.

Car Cleanup

• Remove bugs and tar from cars without damaging the paint by applying a light baking soda paste on a damp cloth. Let it set for 5 minutes, before wiping off the dead bugs and then rinsing clean. Also use to clean chrome trim, bumpers and hubcaps.

• Make your own car wash solution. Combine:
> 1/2 cup liquid detergent
> 1/4 cup baking soda
> 1 gallon water

When washing your car, use one cup of this solution per one pail of warm water.

• Clean car ashtrays with baking soda to make your car smell fresh. In fact, leave a half inch of baking soda at the bottom of the car ash tray to control future cigarette odors.

• Sprinkle baking soda on vinyl seats and scrub them clean with a damp sponge. Rinse with a clean, damp sponge.

• Use baking soda to clean your hands if they are smelly after pumping gas. Sprinkle some right on your hands and wipe them clean with a damp paper towel.

• If you are faced with the results of a bout of car sickness, clean up what you can off the affected area, then cover the area with baking soda to eliminate the odor, neutralize the acid and absorb remaining moisture. Later you can vacuum and shampoo the area.

• Make your car smell good again. Before heading off to the car wash or to use a professional car-vac machine, sprinkle baking soda on fabric seats and carpets. Then just vacuum it up—with the rest of your car's debris—and the car will smell good as well as look good.

Preventive Measures

• Keep a shaker or box of baking soda in your trunk or glove compartment to have available when the occasion arises! Use it as a compact inexpensive extinguisher for a fire—yours or another's.

• Keep baking soda in your earthquake, car or other emergency kit because it can be used for so many things.

Spas and Pools

• Use baking soda to quickly scrub body oils from the sides of a whirlpool tub and from the filter area. It also leaves no scratches on acrylic spa surfaces.

• Clean above-ground pool liners easily with a damp rag and a baking soda paste. The soda even helps keep the pool pH balanced.

• Use baking soda to maintain pH balance in pool water or in a hot tub, to keep water clean and to reduce any eye irritation and burning. Always check disinfectant levels first and add the disinfecting agent as recommend by the manufacturer. Levels should be checked weekly using proper measuring kits.

For those who monitor pH *only* in their pool use the following:

if the pH is:	add (per *10,000 gallons of water*):
less than 7.2	3-4 lbs baking soda
between 7.2 and 7.5	2 lbs baking soda
above 7.5	*don't add any baking soda*

To prevent clouding, especially in hard water areas or when using a calcium chlorinating agent, keep the pH below 7.8 by adding sodium bisulfate or the equivalent, if necessary.

Baking soda can be used to provide *alkalinity* in the proper 80-100 ppm range.

if the alkalinity is:	add *(per 10,000 gallons of water)*:
20 ppm	12 lbs. of baking soda
40 ppm	9 lbs. " "
60 ppm	6 lbs. " "
80 ppm	3 lbs. " "
110 ppm or higher	*don't add any baking soda*

If alkalinity is controlled in the 80-100 ppm, the pH will usually stabilize in its desired range.

Additional information about pool chemistry should be available from your local spa/pool professional. Or you can call ARM & HAMMER® Consumer Relations Division at 1-800-524-1328. *(This service is not available to California residents.)*

CHAPTER THIRTEEN

A GUIDE FOR GREEN THUMBS

How does your garden grow? A whole lot better, says the Green Thumb squad, if there's a box of baking soda handy.

Outdoor Gardens

• For truly magnificent blooms, all flower species which thrive in alkaline soil (geranium, begonia, hydrangea) benefit greatly from occasionally being watered with a weak baking soda solution.

• Sprinkle baking soda lightly on the soil around tomato plants. It sweetens tomatos by lowering their acidity and discourages pests. (*Here's a good place to dispose of that box of baking soda that has served its purpose as a deodorizer in the refrigerator.*)

• Roses resist black spot and powdery mildew if sprayed with the following solution:

> 7 tablespoons baking soda
> a few drops insecticidal soap (*without pyrethrums*)
> 5 gallons water

Spray every other day for a few days but check for signs of burning. If you see none, spray once a week throughout the rest of the rose season.

• Sprinkle baking soda lightly—and just occasionally—around flower beds to discourage rabbits from nibbling on buds.

• Get rid of backyard slugs sprinkling baking soda on them! No need for costly, toxic chemicals.

Make-Your-Own Safe, Organic Pesticides

• Combine:

> 1 teaspoon baking soda
> 1/3 cup cooking oil

From this mixture, measure 2 teaspoons to combine with 1 cup water and fill plant sprayer. This spray is said to kill aphids, spider mites and white flies, and to be benign to beneficial insects.

- Or try:
                2 tablespoons baking soda
                1 gallon water.
  Spray on garden plants.

- For another spray formula option, combine:
                1/2 cup baking soda
                 a few drops liquid detergent
                1 quart water
  Spray occasionally on plants in the early evening to rid them of
  unwanted pests.

- Prevent grass and weeds from growing in sidewalk cracks by
  sprinkling baking soda on the cement and sweeping it into the
  cracks. The excess sodium is what does them in. You can also
  sprinkle baking soda on any other unwanted grass or weeds,
  such as moss growing on patio bricks.

Compost Friendly
- Control compost pile odor with baking soda applied directly
  from the box. It keeps the acidity levels down in the compost
  area.

It's for the Birds
- Clean your bird bath by sprinkling it with baking soda. With a
  damp cloth or brush, scrub away scum. Rinse well and refill
  with water. No toxic residues to be left here.

Indoor Flower/Plant Power
- Clean clay flower pots—inside and out—with baking soda.
  Rinse clean. There is no harmful residue to be absorbed by the
  clay.

• Coat a clay pot with a thin layer of baking soda when transplanting plants, before adding the soil. This helps keeps the dirt fresh for a longer time.

• Dip cut flowers in a solution of baking soda and water to extend their life, rather than using commercial package solutions.

• To clean plants—real or silk—wash them in a solution of 1/2 cup baking soda to 1 gallon cold water. The leaves will shine with no risk of damage.

Controlling Yard Yahoos
• Eliminate outdoor ants in their dirt mounds by first sprinkling baking soda on the mound when it is damp. After a half-hour or so, pour a small amount of vinegar on the ant hill. Ants will ingest the combination and their body enzymes will do the rest.

CHAPTER FOURTEEN

CRAFTS, HOBBIES
AND
OTHER IDEAS FOR FUN

Whenever you sew, or work on a craft project, or set up a model train, or prepare to entertain—you'll be surprised where baking soda can be put to use.

Handicrafts

• Use baking soda, say quilters, as an erasable pattern guide. First use the sewing machine to puncture holes in the pattern paper, tracing the pattern. Then pin the punctured pattern paper on the dark fabric and rub with baking soda. The soda will penetrate the holes, leaving a pattern of dots when the paper is removed. The darker the fabric, the more discernible the baking soda pattern. The same concept can work with sewing patterns.

• Soak soiled needlework, especially plastic canvas objects, in cold water, baking soda, and liquid dish soap. Rinse, and the project looks new.

• Tie a small amount of baking soda in a piece of cloth and run machine and hand sewing needles through the bag to clean the needles.

• Add baking soda to the foam stuffing when you make or recover throw pillows to keep them smelling fresh.

• If you're drying green or wet wood for a craft project, place it in a plastic bag with baking soda for a few days. The latter controls both odor and insects while absorbing moisture.

• Mix baking soda in paints to create an interesting texture. Experiment!

Money Mavens

• Safely clean coins with a paste of baking soda and water. An extremely corroded coin can be cleaned by placing it in a bowl with 2 tablespoons baking soda. Add vinegar until the solution neutralizes. Scrub coins with an old toothbrush. (*WARNING: NOT recommended for investment coin collections.*)

• Clean mildewed paper money by sprinkling it with baking

soda, then placing it between clean pieces of paper (newspaper, book pages, paper toweling, etc.) for a few days.

For the Aficionado

• Sprinkle baking soda between the pages of an old book that has become damp or musty-smelling. It soon smells like new!

• Clean and deodorize band wind instruments such as trumpets or trombones by removing valves and vent pipes and soaking them in baking soda. Allow to dry before reassembling.

• Model train enthusiasts—sprinkle baking soda on your "landscape" to simulate snow.

Holidays and Entertaining

• Direct invited guests to parties using baking soda and a stencil for arrow markings on the road along with your house number. Or use it to create arrows or foot prints down an apartment hallway carpet—to be vacuumed up later. (See page 77 for additional stencil ideas.)

• Set individual candles in small containers filled with a thick paste of baking soda and water. This allows a candle to burn down safely all the way and makes for easy cleanup without scratching or damaging any surface.

• Instead of tinsel on the tree this year, why not let it snow? Pour baking soda into a large shaker bottle and apply it liberally to your tree's branches.

• Keep a box handy for that inevitable wine-on-the-carpet-or-table spill. Dab up excess liquid then sprinkle baking soda on the spot to absorb the wetness and the sodium in it helps neutralize the stain. (See page 44 for more carpet advice.)

CHAPTER FIFTEEN

OUTDOOR FOLKS

Any outing will be less work, more pleasant and more comfortable if you've remembered to bring your trusty box of baking soda along. Bring this book too. It will give you time to review all these fabulous, fun and frugal uses!

RV Campers' and Boaters' Best Bets

• Sprinkle baking soda in picnic coolers, ice chests and beverage coolers to keep them smelling fresh while being stored. The soda is ready to be a cleaner when the next season is upon you.

• Use an open box of baking soda to keep small boat or RV refrigerators smelling sweet, and replace as necessary.

• Place an open box of baking soda in your RV bathroom to dispel odors.

• Flush the water tank of your RV periodically with 1 cup baking soda dissolved in 1 gallon warm water to freshen and sweeten it. Drain and flush with clean water before refilling. Baking soda is compatible with the waste digester/deodorant in holding tanks.

• Sprinkle baking soda throughout your boat before covering it with canvas for winter storage.

• Remember that baking soda is a compact fire extinguisher. When camping extinguish a campfire by tossing handfuls of baking soda at the base of the flames to smother them. (*Before you turn in or leave the campsite, sprinkle embers with water and test the remains with your hands to make sure it's out cold.*) Keep the box of baking soda nearby while cooking in case of flare-ups or flying sparks.

Backpackers and Outdoor Campers

• Be aware that bikers can use a light baking soda/water base paste to insert tubes into tires easily.

• Use baking soda while backpacking: as a tooth cleanser, a deodorant, a salt substitute, an odor eater for hiking boots, a salve for sunburns or campfire burns, an extinguisher to put out campfires, a relief to soothe bug bites, and for washing camp laundry.

- Freshen smelly sleeping bags by sprinkling baking soda inside them. Air them out in the sunshine, too. Shake them out before going to sleep.

- When the damp smell from that last camping trip has clinging power, sprinkle your sleeping bags and tent—inside and out—with baking soda. Shake off excess and store.

Sportsmen/women

- Destroy the human scent in clothes by adding a box of baking soda to the rinse cycle when washing them. (See cooking game tips on page 18.)

- Make some fishing lures spin and jump in the water by filling their hollows with baking soda.

INDEX